A LIFEGUIDE®  BIBLE STUDY

# ACTS

## Seeing God's Power in Action

*24 Studies in 2 Parts for individuals or groups*

**Phyllis J. Le Peau**

With Notes for Leaders

INTERVARSITY PRESS
DOWNERS GROVE, ILLINOIS 60515

*InterVarsity Press® is the book-publishing division of InterVarsity Christian Fellowship®, a student movement active on campus at hundreds of universities, colleges and schools of nursing in the United States of America, and a member movement of the International Fellowship of Evangelical Students. For information about local and regional activities, write Public Relations Dept., InterVarsity Christian Fellowship, 6400 Schroeder Rd., P.O. Box 7895, Madison, WI 53707-7895.*



*Cover photograph: Robert McKendrick*

*ISBN 0-8308-1007-2*

*Printed in the United States of America*

23 22 21 20 19 18 17 16 15 14 13 12 11 10 9

11 10 9 8 7 06 05 04 03 02 01 00 99

# Contents

# Getting the Most from LifeGuide® Bible Studies

Many of us long to fill our minds and our lives with Scripture. We desire to be transformed by its message. LifeGuide® Bible Studies are designed to be an exciting and challenging way to do just that. They help us to be guided by God's Word in every area of life.

### How They Work

LifeGuides have a number of distinctive features. Perhaps the most important is that they are *inductive* rather than *deductive.* In other words, they lead us to *discover* what the Bible says rather than simply *telling* us what it says.

They are also thought provoking. They help us to think about the meaning of the passage so that we can truly understand what the author is saying. The questions require more than one-word answers.

The studies are personal. Questions expose us to the promises, assurances, exhortations and challenges of God's Word. They are designed to allow the Scriptures to renew our minds so that we can be transformed by the Spirit of God. This is the ultimate goal of all Bible study.

The studies are versatile. They are designed for student, neighborhood and church groups. They are also effective for individual study.

### How They're Put Together

LifeGuides also have a distinctive format. Each study need take no more than forty-five minutes in a group setting or thirty minutes in personal study—unless you choose to take more time.

The studies can be used within a quarter system in a church and fit well in a semester or trimester system on a college campus. If a guide has more than thirteen studies, it is divided into two or occasionally three parts of approximately twelve studies each.

LifeGuides use a workbook format. Space is provided for writing answers to each question. This is ideal for personal study and allows group members to prepare in advance for the discussion.

The studies also contain leader's notes. They show how to lead a group discussion, provide additional background information on certain questions, give helpful tips on group dynamics and suggest ways to deal with problems which may arise during the discussion. With such helps, someone with little or no experience can lead an effective study.

**Suggestions for Individual Study**

1. As you begin each study, pray that God will help you to understand and apply the passage to your life.

2. Read and reread the assigned Bible passage to familiarize yourself with what the author is saying. In the case of book studies, you may want to read through the entire book prior to the first study. This will give you a helpful overview of its contents.

3. A good modern translation of the Bible, rather than the King James Version or a paraphrase, will give you the most help. The New International Version, the New American Standard Bible and the Revised Standard Version are all recommended. However, the questions in this guide are based on the New International Version.

4. Write your answers in the space provided in the study guide. This will help you to express your understanding of the passage clearly.

5. It might be good to have a Bible dictionary handy. Use it to look up any unfamiliar words, names or places.

**Suggestions for Group Study**

1. Come to the study prepared. Follow the suggestions for individual study mentioned above. You will find that careful preparation will greatly enrich your time spent in group discussion.

2. Be willing to participate in the discussion. The leader of your group will not be lecturing. Instead, he or she will be encouraging the members of the group to discuss what they have learned from the passage. The leader will be asking the questions that are found in this guide. Plan to share what God has taught you in your individual study.

3. Stick to the passage being studied. Your answers should be based on the verses which are the focus of the discussion and not on outside authorities such as commentaries or speakers. This guide deliberately avoids jumping

from book to book or passage to passage. Each study focuses on only one passage. Book studies are generally designed to lead you through the book in the order in which it was written. This will help you follow the author's argument.

4. Be sensitive to the other members of the group. Listen attentively when they share what they have learned. You may be surprised by their insights! Link what you say to the comments of others so the group stays on the topic. Also, be affirming whenever you can. This will encourage some of the more hesitant members of the group to participate.

5. Be careful not to dominate the discussion. We are sometimes so eager to share what we have learned that we leave too little opportunity for others to respond. By all means participate! But allow others to also.

6. Expect God to teach you through the passage being discussed and through the other members of the group. Pray that you will have an enjoyable and profitable time together.

7. If you are the discussion leader, you will find additional suggestions and helpful ideas for each study in the leader's notes. These are found at the back of the guide.

# Introducing Acts

The book of Acts should come with a warning label reading, "If you are open to God, this witness will call you to new life."

Acts is an extraordinary work. In essence, it is the story of transformed lives—and the difference these lives made in the world.

Just before Acts begins, we see the disciples behind closed doors wallowing in the mire of their craven fear, self-doubt and personal shame. Apart from their master, they were a pathetic group indeed (Jn 20:19; Lk 24:11). However, by the second chapter of Acts, the same men who abandoned Jesus at Gethsemane have become irrepressible dynamos, preaching with utter conviction—and at great personal risk—"the mighty acts of God."

What changed them? And what impact did they make upon their generation and all subsequent ones? *This* is the story of Acts.

Acts is an important book for us today because it confirms that the power which transformed the disciples' lives is the same power that can transform our lives today! That power is, of course, God himself—coming to us through the Holy Spirit.

There are many benefits to studying Acts:

☐ *Acts serves as a distant mirror.* We will see the dynamics of the earliest church, the nature of their fellowship, the intensity of their prayer life, and their out-and-out zeal to declare the saving gospel of Jesus Christ. Through this example, our own situation will be called into question. What does it mean to be the church today—and what are we to be doing?

☐ *Acts emphasizes the primary task of the church—evangelization.* Speaking the gospel is only part of the task. It is the formative process that we see in these earliest communities. In Acts we see the entire process of calling, healing, empowering and sending people forth to love and obey Jesus Christ. Acts will challenge us to a holistic-community spirituality that can renew our churches today.

☐ *Acts calls us to a vital experience with the Holy Spirit.* Jesus promised power to the disciples *after* the Holy Spirit came upon them. And the book of Acts reveals the Holy Spirit as the driving force behind all meaningful ministry in Jesus' name. Where do we look for spiritual power today? education? work? religious heritage? Acts calls us to a Spirit-filled life.

☐ *Acts forges a new sense of identity.* The disciples gradually realized they were no longer Jews (at least from the confessional and ceremonial points-of-view). They slowly began to understand that they were part of that new community of the Spirit which was prophesied in the Hebrew Scriptures. And they saw the need to call all people—Jews and Gentiles—to repentance and fellowship with this new community—the church. Baptism in the name of the Father, the Son and the Holy Spirit, and the Lord's Supper became the outward signs of the inward grace. The emphasis is on relationships.

Through these studies, the explosive power of this living document will touch you. As you work through these studies, may you experience the calling, healing, empowering and sending dynamic of the Holy Spirit.

*Louis Quetel*
*Good Shepherd Lutheran Church*
*Naperville, Illinois*

# *Part 1*
# God's Power in Jerusalem and Judea
### *Acts 1—12*

# 1
# You Will Be My Witnesses
## *Acts 1*

I remember telling a friend, "If I were dying, what I would most need would be confidence that all I believed about Jesus were true. I would want you to read Scripture to me, pray with me, and talk to me about Jesus and heaven." This confidence is not only what I need most when I am dying, but also when I am living.

During the days between his resurrection and ascension, Jesus built the confidence of his disciples. He demonstrated and spoke truth about himself. And then he left them with a clearly defined task and the promise of the power to carry out that task. Thus, Luke was able to write with confidence to Theophilus about Jesus.

---

**1.** When has your faith in Jesus Christ been encouraged by the words of others?

---

**2.** Read Acts 1:1-11. What did Luke, the author of Acts, report to Theophilus about Jesus' last days upon earth?

What gives credibility to this report?

---

**3.** How is your hope and confidence in Jesus affected by what you learn of him in the passage?

---

**4.** Put yourself in the shoes of the apostles. How would you feel if you were the first to be given the task described in verse 8?

---

**5.** How are we equipped for this task, according to the passage?

---

**6.** Imagine that you were there, looking into the sky. How do you think the followers of Jesus were affected by the promise that he would return?

---

**7.** How are you affected by that promise today?

**8.** Read Acts 1:12-26. How did the disciples respond to all that they had seen and heard?

**9.** Why was it important for them to be together?

**10.** How are you affected when you pray with other believers in this way—especially as you consider your part in this task (v. 14)?

**11.** Peter comes forth as the leader of this group. He goes to Scripture immediately when he speaks. How do these words of David affect their confidence as well as give them direction?

**12.** In summary, how does this passage define your task, equip, motivate and give you confidence to complete the task?

# 2
# Receiving the Power
## *Acts 2*

At my school of nursing, a group of upperclassmen wanted to communicate the message of Jesus to the incoming class of freshmen. They realized that there was only one source to accomplish this task—the power of the Holy Spirit. So they decided to pray for each new student by name weeks before they arrived on campus. As a result, many who did not know Jesus when they arrived graduated as maturing Christians.

---

**1.** What do you think it would be like if the Holy Spirit were suddenly withdrawn from the church?

---

**2.** Read Acts 2. Imagine that you were there on the Day of Pentecost. What do you think it would have been like for you as one of the crowd looking on?

---

**3.** How do the Jews respond to the power of the Spirit which they witness?

Why do you think they react this way?

---

**4.** Here, we see Peter as a dynamic leader and preacher. It is the power of the Holy Spirit which has changed this man who was once a coward that denied Jesus three times. Scripture, again, is the foundation of Peter's proclamation of truth. What message does the book of Joel have for the bewildered crowd?

---

**5.** In our study of Acts we will see Peter's perception of evangelism broaden. In this chapter why do you think there is a difference between the people Luke mentions as being present (vv. 9-11) and Peter's address, "Fellow Jews" (v. 15)?

---

**6.** What is there in Peter's sermon that would reassure Theophilus about his faith and help him "know the certainty of the things" that he'd been taught?

---

**7.** What does Peter have to offer to those who are responsive to his message (vv. 37-39)?

**8.** How has your life been affected by the gift of the Holy Spirit?

**9.** Describe the fellowship of the believers in this young church (vv. 42-47).

**10.** What were their priorities?

**11.** How does the life and purpose of your church or Christian fellowship group compare to that of this group?

**12.** In summary, what are all the ways you see the power of the Holy Spirit demonstrated throughout the chapter?

**13.** How does your church or fellowship group need to change in order to see the power of the Holy Spirit demonstrated in these ways?

# 3
# Healing Power
## *Acts 3*

I met Anne at the hospital where I was working one evening. She was in an isolation room. She had hepatitis from using contaminated needles to take drugs.

In time our relationship grew, and Anne came to know Jesus. She recovered from hepatitis and went off drugs. She worked at healing her relationship with her parents. Later, she married and established a Christian home.

Anne's story makes it clear that the power of the Holy Spirit is not only demonstrated through physical healing, but also in the "complete healing" that includes every aspect of our lives.

---

**1.** In your experience what causes non-Christians to be open to hearing about Jesus?

---

**2.** Read Acts 3. The outreach in Jerusalem continues as Peter and John respond to a crippled beggar. What is the significance of the fact that they found him at the temple gate?

**3.** What happened that caused the people to be filled with wonder and amazement (vv. 1-10)?

**4.** How does the response of the people to this miracle contrast with that of the beggar (vv. 8 and 11-12)?

**5.** When Peter saw the response of the crowd, he saw his opportunity and talked to them about Jesus. According to Peter's message, what had God done to Jesus (vv. 13-15)?

What had the Jews done to him?

**6.** How is the authority of Jesus demonstrated in this miracle (v. 16)?

**7.** What do you think it meant that "complete healing" (v. 16) was given to the beggar?

What healing do you need in your life?

---

**8.** How did Peter explain that all that had happened to Jesus was a part of God's plan (vv. 17-26)?

---

**9.** The wait for Jesus to return from heaven may seem very long. How is your perspective on this wait affected by verse 21?

---

**10.** How do you respond when you have opportunities like Peter's to talk about Jesus?

---

**11.** In summary, how is the power of the Holy Spirit linked to the truth about Jesus in this passage?

---

**12.** The "completely" healed man was a powerful testimony to the power of God and the truth of Peter's words. How have you seen the power of God demonstrated in your life and in the lives of others?

# 4
# Called into Question

## *Acts 4:1-31*

A disabled person becomes abled! And a one-time burden to society, a beggar, becomes functional and a contributing citizen!

How do the religious leaders respond to these miraculous events? Instead of expressing gratitude, they become extremely upset. The two men responsible for the healing are arrested.

---

**1.** When has your faith in Jesus Christ been challenged by others?

---

**2.** Read Acts 4:1-22. What has upset the religious leaders (vv. 1-2)?

What action did they take (vv. 3-7)?

---

**3.** Just a few weeks have passed since Annas and Caiaphas had been involved in the condemnation of Jesus. In his response to their question "By what power or what name did you do this?" Peter is forcing them to encounter Jesus again. What does Peter say about him (vv. 10-12)?

---

**4.** In what ways does the church confront the world with Jesus Christ today?

How does the church fail to do this?

---

**5.** In verses 13-22 what all made it so difficult for the opposing religious leaders to bring this unacceptable behavior to a halt?

---

**6.** How do these same things, when present in our Christian communities, enhance accomplishing the task of spreading the news about Jesus?

---

**7.** Imagine that you had been in a group of believers John and Peter returned to and told of what had happened. What would have been your reaction?

---

**8.** Read Acts 4:23-31. What was the reaction of the believers to John and Peter's account?

**9.** What is the significance of their unity in the midst of their task and power being challenged?

---

**10.** What does their prayer tell you about their faith in the character, power and faithfulness of God?

---

**11.** How does the quote from Psalm 2 clearly demonstrate God's character, faithfulness and power?

---

**12.** What did they finally request of God in the last part of their prayer?

---

**13.** "After they prayed, the place where they were meeting was shaken. And they were all filled with the Holy Spirit and spoke the word of God boldly." In what ways do you need the power of the Holy Spirit to face the world today?

---

Ask God to fill you with the Spirit as you face constant challenge to the power for and the task of experiencing and communicating the gospel.

# 5
# Oneness of Heart

## *Acts 4:32—5:16*

It was with a heavy feeling of dread and pain that I read name after name engraved on the Vietnam Memorial in Washington, D.C. Then, I saw that next to the memorial stands a statue of three men—a Black, a Hispanic and a White soldier. They were standing *very close together.*

The tour guide, a former soldier who fought in Nam, explained the significance of the statue. He said that there were more minorities fighting for the U.S. than ever before. And the reason that they were standing so close together was that in Vietnam they learned, like never before, how very much they *needed each other.*

In this study we will see that when the battle is spiritual, our need for each other is even more critical.

---

**1.** When have you experienced the power of the Holy Spirit in your own life as a result of being at one with other believers?

---

**2.** Read Acts 4:32—5:16. How is oneness of heart and mind demonstrated in 4:32-37?

**3.** What have Ananias and Sapphira done that is not consistent with Christian community (5:1-2)?

---

**4.** Pretend you are watching the interaction between Peter and Ananias and Sapphira (5:3-9). How would you report this incident?

---

**5.** Verse 11 states that "great fear seized the whole church and all who heard about these events." How do you think the church was affected by this fear?

---

**6.** How does this story demonstrate the high value that God places on truth and unity within the body of Christ?

---

**7.** In what ways do we lie to each other today within our Christian communities?

---

**8.** How do these practices of untruth bring about death, in a spiritual and emotional sense, within our communities?

**9.** What are the tangible evidences of the power of the Holy Spirit in this community in 5:12-16?

---

**10.** Why do you suppose that no one dared to join the believers when they met together in Solomon's Colonnade?

---

**11.** What difference would it make in our witness to the world today if believers were "highly regarded by the people"?

---

**12.** What characteristics does your Christian community share with the believers in Acts?

How is it different?

---

**13.** How could you begin to help others in your church or fellowship understand what Christian community is about?

# 6
# Persecution and Expansion
## *Acts 5:17—6:7*

In 1956 tragic news spread across the world. Five American men—sons, husbands and fathers—were massacred by a tribe of Auca Indians. Their purpose was to take the good news of Jesus Christ to the Aucas. The opposition to this endeavor cost them their lives.

That agonizing loss, which seemed at the time to be such a waste, has turned into great fruit for the kingdom of God. Over the years that same tribe of Indians has been transformed by the power of God. The message of Jesus was taken to them by the loved ones of those five young men. Another visible fruit of this great loss is the many who have gone into the world with the gospel, having been inspired by the lives and deaths of these missionaries. The church of Jesus Christ continues to expand today in spite of great persecution, even as it did in the day of the apostles.

---

**1.** When have you encountered internal and/or external opposition when you have attempted to proclaim the message of Jesus?

Which is more difficult for you to deal with? Why?

**2.** Read Acts 5:17-42. List the expressions of, and causes of, emotion throughout this passage.

---

**3.** Describe the apostles' response, motivation and source of strength throughout this whole episode.

---

**4.** In what ways do you sense a need for this kind of response, motivation and drawing upon the strength of the Holy Spirit in your life?

in the life of your Christian community?

---

**5.** What was Gamaliel's message to the religious leaders (vv. 34-39)?

---

**6.** How was his influence in saving the apostles' lives an example of that truth which he spoke?

**7.** Read Acts 6:1-7. As the number of disciples increased, what practical needs began to present themselves?

---

**8.** How did the Twelve respond to these needs (6:2-6)?

---

**9.** How does this response demonstrate sensitivity to these needs, and their commitment to God's primary direction to them?

---

**10.** How does this response to need compare and contrast to your Christian community?

---

**11.** What is the spirit of those who are involved in the work of God throughout this passage?

What is the response to the truth that is being lived and proclaimed?

---

**12.** As you observe the work of the Holy Spirit throughout these passages, what actions do you think you and/or your group should take to insure his ministry among you?

# 7
# Stephen, Full of Spirit and Wisdom

## *Acts 6:8—7:60*

I am glad for those people in my life who make me long to know God better. God's character in them makes me hunger and thirst for him. That is what happens to me when I am exposed to Stephen. I read about him and I want to know God.

Stephen is described as "full of the Holy Spirit and wisdom, full of God's grace and power." He was a gift to the early church but could not be tolerated by her enemies.

---

**1.** Think of a person that makes you want to know God better. What is that person like?

---

**2.** Read Acts 6:8—7:60. What do you learn about Stephen throughout this passage?

---

**3.** What do you think it was like when the religious leaders could not stand up against his wisdom or the Spirit by whom he spoke?

---

**4.** What do the accusations against Stephen tell us about why the Jewish religious leaders were so upset (6:13-14)?

---

**5.** Sometimes the speech in chapter 7 is called "Stephen's defense," although it is actually a defense of pure Christianity as God's appointed way to worship. What are the main points of this defense?

---

**6.** What did God tell Abraham would happen to his descendants, the Hebrews (7:1-7)?

---

**7.** How are you affected when you see all that God told Abraham would happen to the Hebrews, years before it happened, even before he had a *son,* unfold in history?

**8.** What implications is Stephen making about where God can be worshiped in 7:44-50?

---

**9.** What direct application does Stephen make concerning the religious leaders from 7:39-43 (see 7:51-53)?

---

**10.** How did God directly minister to Stephen as he faced the angry leaders and his own death?

---

**11.** Throughout this whole passage, we see in Stephen the evidence of being full of Spirit and wisdom. What are the evidences today of being full of Spirit and wisdom?

---

**12.** In what aspect of your life would you like to reflect more Spirit and wisdom?

---

Ask God to fill you with Spirit and wisdom.

# 8

# The Power of Suffering

## *Acts 8:1-40*

Stephen is dead. When he is buried, the people mourn deeply. The church has experienced the tragedy of her first martyr.

In this study we meet Philip and Saul. Saul approves of Stephen's death. He is putting all his energy into destroying the rest of Jesus' followers. In contrast, Philip is one of the seven, full of the Spirit and wisdom. His energy goes into the proclamation of the truth about Jesus. People respond.

And so both the persecution and the expansion of the church continue.

---

**1.** What do you feel you need to become a more effective witness for Jesus?

---

**2.** Read Acts 8. In this passage the command to be witnesses in all of Judea and Samaria (Acts 1:8) is fulfilled. What are the causes and extent of the spread of the gospel at this time?

**3.** How does the power of the Holy Spirit continue to be demonstrated?

---

**4.** Look at the story of Simon the Sorcerer (vv. 9-25). How does he attempt to get spiritual power?

What is his motivation for wanting this power (vv. 18-19)?

---

**5.** In contrast, what is God's way for his people to receive spiritual power (vv. 20-23)?

---

**6.** The story of Simon the Sorcerer demonstrates that becoming a Christian does not instantly resolve all problems and character flaws. What do you learn from Peter concerning nurturing young believers?

What results do you see in Simon?

**7.** What are the factors involved in the eunuch's coming to know the Lord (vv. 26-39)?

**8.** How was Philip's ministry to the eunuch the beginning of the witness "to the ends of the earth" (Acts 1:8)?

**9.** Today we refer to different kinds of evangelism, such as friendship evangelism, mass evangelism, door-to-door evangelism and literature evangelism. What kinds of evangelism do you see in this passage?

**10.** What principles of evangelism have you observed throughout this study?

**11.** What have you learned from this passage that might make you a more effective witness for Jesus?

# 9
# Saul's Conversion

## *Acts 9:1-31*

When Chuck Colson became a Christian in prison, the whole nation reacted with skepticism—Christians and non-Christians alike. Of all the leading characters in the Watergate scandal, he was one of the most notorious. Could such a calculating man sincerely come to God?

---

**1.** Whose conversion to Christianity has been most astonishing to you? Why?

---

**2.** Read Acts 9:1-31. Review what you know about Saul (7:58—8:3). What further insights do you get about him from 9:1-2?

---

**3.** Describe Saul's encounter with Jesus Christ in verses 3-9. What is the emotional, spiritual, physical and social climate?

---

**4.** Ananias is the second person within three days to have a direct encounter with the Lord. Compare and contrast his encounter (vv. 10-16) with that of Saul's.

**5.** What is the significance of Ananias addressing Saul as "Brother" (v. 17)?

**6.** What do you learn about obedience to God through Saul and Ananias?

**7.** What does Saul's conversion teach us about those in our life who are most likely *not* to believe?

**8.** Consider the people in your life who are most antagonistic to Christianity. How might God use you to bring them to Christ?

**9.** What is the response of both believers and non-believers to Saul and his ministry (vv. 19-30)?

**10.** What role does Barnabas play in Saul's life and ministry?

**11.** Barnabas means "Son of Encouragement" (4:36). When have you experienced someone's being a Barnabas to you and/or you to another?

**12.** How would you like to grow as a person who communicates the gospel to those who are antagonistic to it?

# 10
# Salvation for Every Nation
## *Acts 9:32—10:48*

Once the Berlin Wall seemed impenetrable, and communism powerful and indestructible. For seventy years, Christians wondered if Christmas would ever again be openly celebrated in Russia.

Then, dramatically, the wall fell. Communism collapsed. Nations that had been closed to the gospel for years began to welcome Christians, their help and their message with open arms.

The historic breakthrough was like the one the early Christians experienced in this passage. A seemingly impenetrable spiritual wall was broken down. In both situations we see that from God's perspective there is always the potential for reaching every person in all the corners of the world with the wonderful news of Jesus Christ.

---

**1.** When have you felt separated from people because of cultural or racial differences?

---

**2.** Read Acts 9:32—10:48. How is God's power demonstrated in 9:32-43?

**3.** This is the first time Peter has been involved in raising someone from the dead. How might this help prepare him for what happens in chapter 10?

---

**4.** How did God prepare Cornelius for Peter (10:1-8)?

---

**5.** According to 10:4, what caused God to take notice of Cornelius?

---

**6.** To what extent are prayer and giving to the poor priorities for you?

---

**7.** In what ways did God prepare Peter for Cornelius (10:9-33)?

---

**8.** What evidence is there that Cornelius expected God to work (10:24-26)?

**9.** What lessons do we learn from Cornelius' life?

**10.** Throughout the chapter, we see Peter in process concerning God's desire for him to take the gospel to the Gentiles. Trace the process of Peter's understanding.

**11.** What would have been the consequences if Cornelius or Peter had not obeyed God?

**12.** In summary, how do you see God's purpose, as stated in Acts 1:8, "You will receive power when the Holy Spirit comes on you; and you will be my witnesses in Jerusalem, and in all Judea and Samaria, and to the ends of the earth," being fulfilled in this passage?

**13.** In what ways do you need to grow in relating to people of other cultures and races?

# 11
# The First Jewish-Gentile Church
## *Acts 11*

Luke set up the stories of Peter and Cornelius and Ananias and Saul with amazing symmetry. The Holy Spirit simultaneously prepared the heart of Ananias and of Saul—as he simultaneously prepared those of Peter and Cornelius. Peter questioned and hesitated, as did Ananias. Peter doubted whether he could be friends with the Gentiles. Ananias whether he could approach the enemy of the church. Both obey without hesitation when God makes his divine will known.

These stories come together in today's study. Peter defends his ministry to Cornelius to the church at Jerusalem. He convinces them of God's work in the Gentiles. It is also here that Saul, that one-time enemy of the church, reappears as a *minister* to the church in Antioch, a church filled with both Jew and Gentile Christians.

---

**1.** When have you been criticized by other Christians for doing what was right?

---

**2.** Read Acts 11:1-30. What kind of reception was awaiting Peter when he went back up to Jerusalem?

**3.** What are you like when someone criticizes you?

**4.** What can we learn from the way Peter responded to his critics?

**5.** What seemed to be the final and most convincing proof to Peter of God's working in the Gentiles (vv. 15-17)? Why?

**6.** What kinds of evidence of new life do you look for in new believers?

**7.** In the meantime the gospel is spreading to Gentiles at a tremendous rate in Antioch. What kind of care is provided for new believers (vv. 22-30)?

**8.** What was the reason for, and the results of, Barnabas's trip to Antioch (vv. 22-30)?

**9.** How does our care for new believers compare and contrast to the care given here?

---

**10.** How do you see in this passage the true meaning of "Christian" being more fully discovered and lived out in a multicultural church?

---

**11.** How does your church and Christian community need to experience this more?

# 12
# Miraculous Escape
## *Acts 12*

Hudson Taylor, famous missionary to China, said, "Man is moved by God through prayer alone." We see the power of God demonstrated in this passage in response to the prayers of his people.

**1.** How have you seen God respond to a group of people who were earnestly praying?

**2.** Read Acts 12:1-25. Describe the main characters in this passage.

How do they each respond to what is happening to and around them?

**3.** What seems to motivate Herod's actions (vv. 1-5)?

**4.** What does the church's response to James's death and Peter's being in prison (vv. 5 and 12) demonstrate about prayer?

**5.** Think about Peter's escape from prison. How would you have been affected if you were Peter?

---

**6.** Why do you think the praying Christians reacted as they did to Peter's return?

---

**7.** When have you been like those who told Rhoda, "You're out of your mind" (v. 15)?

---

**8.** Why was Herod struck down (vv. 21-23)?

---

**9.** Contrast Herod's end with what happened with the Word of God (vv. 19-24).

---

**10.** The earnest prayer of the church significantly affected the outcome of events in this chapter. How is your motivation to pray influenced by this truth?

---

**11.** Summarize chapters 1—12 by listing the themes that have run throughout the chapters and what you have learned about these themes.

**Part 2**

# God's Power at the Ends of the Earth

**Acts 13—28**

# 1
# Paul's First Missionary Journey
## *Acts 13—14*

Peter has disappeared. We do not know where he is hiding. Luke is ushering Peter from the stage, while Paul steps to the forefront. Peter, the apostle to the Jews, has played his part well and prepared the way for Paul, the apostle to the Gentiles.

Paul and Barnabas have completed their mission of mercy in Jerusalem on behalf of the church at Antioch (11:29) and have returned to Antioch with John Mark. In this study we will look at Paul's first missionary journey—the beginning of his master plan of evangelism.

---

**1.** Think of someone you know who effectively shares the gospel. What qualities do you see in that person?

---

**2.** Read Acts 13—14. Antioch was the second great metropolis of the church and the mother of Gentile Christianity. What role did the church of Antioch play in Paul's first missionary journey (13:1-3; 14:26-28)?

**3.** In missionary outreach how do churches today compare and/or contrast with those of Antioch?

**4.** Review Paul's message in the synagogue in Pisidian Antioch (13:16-41). What truths of the gospel are communicated?

**5.** How does Paul's message show sensitivity to his audience and the context?

In what relationships and situations do you need this same sensitivity?

**6.** List the different responses to the gospel (13:7-8, 13, 42-45, 48, 52; 14:1-5) that you see throughout this passage.

**7.** How did Paul respond to those who rejected the gospel (13:9-11, 46, 51)?

to those who believed (14:9-10, 21-23)?

**8.** In this passage the response to the gospel by believers was to be filled with "joy and the Holy Spirit" (13:52). How prevalent is this in the life of our church today? Explain.

**9.** People today are not apt to offer sacrifices to those who bring the good news of Jesus. However, in what ways are we faced with the temptation to be "god" in another's life or to take credit for what God has done?

**10.** How can we help one another when in the midst of such temptations?

**11.** As you look over these two chapters and Paul's first journey, what qualities do you see in him and in Barnabas that made them effective in their ministry?

**12.** Which of these qualities do you want God to develop in you to make you more effective in communicating the gospel?

# 2
# Conflict in the Church
## *Acts 15*

In most areas of life, I think I am pretty realistic. When it comes to conflict among believers, however, I tend to be an idealist. I believe that unity is something that God requires of us. Believers should be able to talk, pray and work through conflict—just the way it was worked through by the church at Jerusalem.

However, I am becoming a little more realistic about this. I have experienced several situations in which I felt like I did everything within my power to bring about reconciliation—but failed.

This seems to be the case with Paul and Barnabas. These two men who were used by God to keep a church from splitting could not resolve their own differences and ended up going separate ways. The late Kenneth Strachan of the Latin America Mission said, "We all need to live and serve in the constant recognition of our own humanity."

---

**1.** What are you like when you are in strong disagreement with others?

---

**2.** Read Acts 15:1-35. Describe the conflict that arises between the Christians in this passage.

**3.** Describe the spirit of those involved and the steps that were taken to resolve this conflict.

---

**4.** What were the results?

---

**5.** What principles do you observe that are vital to follow as we face conflict with others in our Christian community?

---

**6.** Which of these principles do you struggle with implementing the most?

---

**7.** Read Acts 15:36-41. In what ways do you see (or can you assume) unity between Paul and Barnabas?

---

**8.** What was the cause of their conflict?

**9.** Paul and Barnabas came to the point of "agreeing to disagree" and going their separate ways. What were the benefits of this temporary solution?

---

**10.** Both Paul and Barnabas seemed to have strong cases for their points of view. Under what kinds of circumstances should we surrender deep convictions when they are challenged by another?

---

**11.** No matter how strongly we feel about an issue, we do not see the whole picture. How should that fact affect *the way* we respond to people with whom we are in conflict with?

---

**12.** When you are in conflict with others how does your response compare or contrast with that of Paul and Barnabas?

with the leaders of the church (vv. 1-35)?

---

**13.** How would you like to become more like them in your responses when in conflict?

# 3
# What Must I Do?
## *Acts 16*

The memory is still vivid. The event was InterVarsity's Urbana Missionary Conference. The place—a dormitory room. The person, a young lady from the Bible study group I led.

I sensed the prompting of the Holy Spirit to stop by Susan's room. As I walked in to say "hi" she looked up from the booklet she was reading and said, "I would like to become a Christian. Will you help me?"

This dormitory setting was not quite as dramatic as the Philippian jail. But it was just as exciting to hear Susan's words, as it was for Paul and Silas to hear the jailer's cry, "Sirs, what must I do to be saved?"

---

**1.** What makes it easier for you to obey God?

What makes you hesitate?

---

**2.** Read Acts 16:1-10. In verses 6-10 how is Paul directed concerning where he should go?

**3.** What principles of guidance do you see here?

---

**4.** When have you experienced God's leading in this way?

---

**5.** Read Acts 16:11-40. Paul responded immediately to God's message. How was his obedience confirmed on arriving in Macedonia?

---

**6.** There are many reasons that people reject the gospel. Material gain is the reason for the opposition to the gospel on the part of the owners of the slave girl in verse 19. What are reasons that you see today for rejecting the truth?

---

**7.** The slave owners had Paul and Silas jailed. Their response to being in jail and being beaten was to pray and sing hymns. Describe the events of the night that led up to the jailor's question "What must I do to be saved?" (vv. 23-30).

---

**8.** How does your response to opposition to and suffering for the gospel compare and contrast to that of Paul and Silas (v. 25)?

**9.** Paul and Silas speak the truth of the gospel as well as living it out. How do you give both a verbal and a living witness to Jesus?

---

**10.** It is clear in the book of Acts that God is concerned about the world and the nations being reached with the gospel. But he is also concerned about reaching individuals. What individuals were affected by Paul's obedience to God's leading (vv. 14, 18, 30-31)? How?

---

**11.** What might have been the consequences of Paul's ignoring God's call to Macedonia?

---

**12.** Is there a person or task to whom God is calling you?

What steps do you need to take for immediate and unreserved obedience?

# 4
# An Unknown God

## *Acts 17*

Only a few short decades ago, Christians in the West could assume that most people they met belonged to a church or at least based their lives on Judeo-Christian values. Today, Christians in the West face what Christians in the East have had to cope with for centuries—a wide variety of religious beliefs and practices that often have little in common with Christianity. The world's major religions, Hinduism, Buddhism and Islam, are making inroads as are a variety of cults, New Age philosophies, occultic activities and even traditional paganism.

How do we cope with a world that knows or cares so little about the truth of Jesus Christ? Paul left us a helpful model when he visited the world center of pagan philosophy and religion—Athens.

---

**1.** What kinds of philosophies do you encounter as you attempt to communicate the gospel in our modern world?

---

**2.** Read Acts 17:1-34. In this chapter Paul interacts with three cities and three different cultures. Compare and contrast Paul's ministry in Thessalonica and Berea. (What approach did he take? How was his message received by the people? What kinds of results did he have?)

**3.** In Thessalonica and Berea, as in most places, Paul makes his contacts in the synagogues and speaks almost exclusively from Scripture. How does his ministry in Athens differ from this?

---

**4.** How do the people respond to his teaching in Athens?

---

**5.** In his lecture in Athens Paul mentions "the objects of your worship." What are some of the objects of worship for people in our culture?

---

**6.** How does the message of Christ speak to these objects of worship?

---

**7.** In Athens Paul begins to tell them about the living God with an inscription from one of their altars—"to an unknown god." What are "points of truth" from which you can start from to communicate the gospel to those in your world?

---

**8.** Paul's different approaches show his understanding of the culture and his willingness to communicate with people where they are. What different kinds of approaches are needed to touch those God has placed in your world with the gospel?

---

**9.** Though Paul approaches people differently, some points in the content of his message are very consistent. Identify these (vv. 3, 18, 24-28, 30-31).

---

**10.** What are ways that you might be tempted to compromise the message of the gospel as you communicate it to certain people?

---

**11.** How do you need to better prepare yourself to effectively communicate the gospel of Jesus Christ to those to whom God has called you to minister?

# 5
# Companions in Ministry

## *Acts 18*

Just recently, I visited my childhood pastor and his wife. As I left them, my heart was full of gratitude. Gratitude not only for the Wrights, but also for the others past and present who have prepared me for outreach. I am thankful for those who have prayed for me, been my friends, walked along with me, listened to me, loved me and cared about my walk with God and my service to others, who have encouraged me and corrected me. I enjoy thinking about the people who have touched my life and who have been companions in ministry.

I am not alone in this need for companionship. In this study we will look at some of the people in Paul's life who were his companions in ministry.

---

**1.** When have you felt alone in the ministry of bringing others to Christ?

What makes you feel alone?

---

**2.** Read Acts 18:1-28. List the people in Paul's life that you see in this passage.

**3.** Let's look more closely at some of these relationships. What was the significance of his relationship with Priscilla and Aquila (vv. 2-4, 18-19)?

---

**4.** What did Silas and Timothy contribute to Paul's life and ministry?

---

**5.** When have you been sustained by someone's bringing you good news of God's work elsewhere, entering into your ministry, sharing themselves or their home with you or supporting you financially or in other ways?

---

**6.** What keeps you from allowing others to enter into your life and ministry in such ways?

---

**7.** Contrast the response of the Jews in Corinth (vv. 4-6) to that of Crispus and his household (vv. 7-8).

---

**8.** Why do you think God chose to speak to Paul with words of comfort at this time (vv. 9-11)?

How was his ministry affected by God's words?

---

**9.** In verses 18-23 what do you learn about Paul's relationships?

---

**10.** Describe Apollos (vv. 24-26).

---

**11.** What did he need that Aquila and Priscilla were able to give to him?

---

**12.** How was Apollos' ministry affected by his relationship with them (vv. 27-28)?

---

**13.** As you review this passage, what ways do you recognize in which you need to develop, build and nurture relationships that will contribute to your spiritual growth and outreach?

# 6
# In the Name of Jesus

## *Acts 19:1—20:12*

We left Paul in chapter 18 traveling throughout Galatia and Phrygia "strengthening all the disciples." In this chapter he returns to Ephesus, where he settles for two and a half years.

Great work is done there during this time, and it radiates out to other cities in the province of Asia. Luke vividly portrays the effect of Paul's ministry in just a few scenes in this chapter.

---

**1.** How would you like to see the power of God revealed in your Christian community?

---

**2.** Read Acts 19. Scan the passage and describe the incidences where you see God's power revealed.

---

**3.** Wherever the gospel is communicated with effectiveness there will be both positive and negative responses. What are the positive results throughout this passage?

What are the negative responses?

---

**4.** In 19:1-7 Paul encounters some disciples. What is his concern for them?

What did he do to interact with them effectively?

---

**5.** What do you see in Paul's relationship with the disciples that might help you in relating to young Christians or your non-Christian friends?

---

**6.** Throughout this entire passage it is evident that Paul has a strategy for communicating the gospel. Specifically, what strategy does Paul have for his ministry in Ephesus (19:8-10)?

---

**7.** What kind of plan for communicating the gospel would be helpful in your world?

What would you like to see happen?

---

**8.** What happened with the Jews who were driving out evil spirits in the name of Jesus (19:11-14)? Why?

---

**9.** How did this become a testimony to the power of God (19:15-20)?

---

**10.** What is the cause of the riot in Ephesus (vv. 23-41)?

How was it settled?

---

**11.** Read Acts 20:1-12. Paul continued to travel and encourage believers as he preached the gospel. What effect did the episode in 20:7-12 have on the crowd?

---

**12.** What "modern day" positive responses have you seen as a result of the gospel being communicated with power?

negative responses?

---

**13.** How can you prepare yourself for both positive and negative responses as you are a part of communicating the gospel of Christ?

# 7
# Paul's Farewell

## *Acts 20:13-38*

I will see you in heaven." I nodded, gave him a hug and a kiss and walked away from his bedside. When I left the room, I wept.

Although it was twenty years ago that I said goodby to Pop Z, the memory is still deep in my heart.

In this chapter we will enter into weeping as Paul says his final goodby to the elders at Ephesus. He knows that more hardship and prison await him in Jerusalem. And he will never see the faces of these elders again.

---

**1.** Imagine what it would like to say goodby to someone knowing that you would never see them again. Describe your thoughts and feelings.

---

**2.** Read Acts 20:13-38. What do you feel as you read through this passage?

---

**3.** What does Paul say about his ministry to the Ephesians (vv. 18-21, 26-27, 31, 33-35)?

**4.** Which of these do you want to be able to say at the end of your own life? Why?

---

**5.** What steps do you need to take now in order to be able to do so?

---

**6.** What are Paul's priorities (vv. 22-25)?

---

**7.** How do your priorities compare and contrast with his?

---

**8.** What instructions did Paul give to the leaders of the church at Ephesus (vv. 28-31)?

---

**9.** According to verse 32, why can Paul leave them with confidence?

**10.** In summary, according to this passage, why would Paul be able to say with integrity and humility to these leaders, "Follow my example. Do as I have done"?

---

**11.** Who is in your spiritual care?

---

**12.** How are you preparing those that you nurture spiritually so that you can leave them with this same confidence?

---

**13.** Paul and the Ephesian elders were given the rare and special gift of being able to say goodby. What would you want to say to those in your spiritual care if you knew that you were going to die?

Take time to express your hope and your love to that person in the near future.

# 8 Facing Opposition

## *Acts 21:1—22:21*

Five young men sang:

"We rest on Thee—our Shield and our Defender!
We go not forth alone against the foe;
Strong in Thy strength, safe in Thy keeping tender,
We rest on Thee and in Thy name we go.

"Yea, in Thy name, O Captain of salvation!
In Thy dear Name, all other names above;
Jesus our Righteousness, our sure foundation,
Our Prince of glory and our King of love.

"We go in faith, our own great weakness feeling,
And needing more each day Thy grace to know:
Yet from our hearts a song of triumph pealing;
We rest on Thee, and in Thy name we go.

"We rest on Thee our Shield and our Defender!
Thine is the battle, Thine shall be the praise
When passing through the gates of pearly splendor,
Victors—we rest with Thee, through endless days."

as they went to their death, taking the gospel of Jesus Christ to the Auca Indians. Like Paul, knowing that death was a very real possibility, they did not turn aside from what they knew God wanted them to do.

**1.** When have you been warned that something you were about to do could be dangerous?

How did you feel?

---

**2.** Read Acts 21:1-26. Describe the warnings to Paul concerning going to Jerusalem (vv. 4, 10-12).

---

**3.** How did Paul respond to these warnings (vv. 5, 13)?

---

**4.** How do you think those observing Paul were affected by his single-mindedness?

---

**5.** Think of a person you know who is focused on obeying God. How are you affected by his/her obedience?

---

**6.** Paul arrives in Jerusalem, is greeted by the elders and reports what God has done through his ministry. What are the elders concerned about for Paul (vv. 20-25)?

**7.** How does Paul demonstrate his desire to be at one with the Jewish Christians (v. 26)?

---

**8.** Read Acts 21:27—22:21. Note how Paul was treated with mob hysteria, assumption and false evidence (21:27-36, 38). How does he respond to all of this (21:37—22:21)?

---

**9.** Let's look more closely at his defense. What is the significance of his addressing the listeners as "brothers and fathers"?

---

**10.** What other qualities do you see in this defense?

---

**11.** How do you usually respond when you find yourself in conflict because of obedience to God?

---

**12.** What have you seen in this passage that will help you become more single-minded in your obedience to God's will?

# 9
# God at Work

## *Acts 22:22—23:35*

Being under God's protection is not a guarantee of physical safety. Being under his protection does guarantee that our Father is with us, has purpose for us and that nothing happens to us that does not come through his hands. We can live with confidence that our life on earth will not end until that purpose for us is complete. And that ultimately we will end up safe and protected in heaven. Paul was so sure of God's hand in his life that he continued to move out boldly with the message of Jesus Christ in spite of physical danger intensifying.

---

**1.** What are ways that you've seen God working in someone's life?

---

**2.** Read Acts 22:22—23:35. Throughout this passage, we can see God's hand in the circumstances of Paul's life, protecting and directing him. In Acts 22:22-29 what is the source of the conflict?

What is it that protects Paul?

**3.** In 23:1-10 what is the source of the conflict?

How is Paul protected?

---

**4.** Why was Paul struck on the mouth for saying, "My brothers, I have fulfilled my duty to God in all good conscience to this day" (23:1)?

What was he claiming about himself?

---

**5.** What would you say is your purpose in life?

---

**6.** In Acts 23:12-25 the Jews are frustrated because they cannot get rid of Paul through the law, so they decide to ambush and kill him on their own. How is Paul protected?

---

**7.** We have observed God's protection of Paul. How do we see God's care for Paul in a more direct and supernatural way in 23:11?

**8.** Think about God's hand in your life and ministry. How have you seen him work to protect and direct you toward his will?

**9.** What do you learn about Claudius Lysias in Acts 23:23-30?

**10.** How does Claudius Lysias present a picture of our own human nature?

**11.** In what ways do you need to grow in humbly acknowledging God's hand in your life?

**12.** How has your hope for God's will to be done in you been affected by looking at God's hand in Paul's life?

# 10
# Falsely Accused
## Acts 24:1—25:12

Our dear friend George was falsely accused and on trial for heresy. My husband prayed fervently that God would shut their mouths, that he would bind their efforts, and that truth would prevail and bring freedom. He asked God to confound their actions so that their own words would bring out the truth and show up their false accusations.

God chose to do what Andy asked for . . . and George was exonerated in a dramatic fashion. The words of the accusers brought condemnation on them. The defense did not even have to present their case.

The pain, however, in being falsely accused is great. And the damage was not easily repaired. But George's consistent godly response throughout the whole ordeal reminded me of Jesus and Paul when they were falsely accused.

---

**1.** How do you usually respond when you are falsely accused?

---

**2.** Read Acts 24:1-27. What are the accusations brought against Paul by the Jews?

**3.** What does the extent of the flattery lavished upon Felix tell you about the accusers?

---

**4.** How would you describe Paul's defense? (Consider the content and the attitude and tone.)

---

**5.** What do you think is the significance of the fact that Felix was well acquainted with the Way (v. 22)?

---

**6.** Why do you think Felix responded to the gospel as he did?

---

**7.** When have you known someone to respond to the proclamation of the gospel as Felix did?

What might this mean?

---

**8.** Read Acts 25:1-12. Two years have passed since his trial, and Festus has become the new governor. The Jews have not given up. They continue to plot to kill Paul and ask Festus to have him transferred to Jerusalem. Festus refuses and tells the Jewish leaders to come to Caesarea for the trial. What evidence is there in this passage that Festus knows that Paul is innocent?

---

**9.** Why does Festus suggest that Paul go back to Jerusalem to be on trial?

---

**10.** How does Paul respond? Why?

---

**11.** Describe a time you have been falsely accused because of your faith.

---

**12.** What can you learn about how to respond to accusers from the way Paul responded to his accusers?

# 11
# Testimony Before Agrippa
## *Acts 25:13—26:32*

Though his innocence has been clearly stated many times, Paul remains a prisoner. He repeatedly has to face the unfair charges of the Jewish leaders. He has made his defense with integrity and power, and in return he gets only threats of death.

In it all Paul's witness remains consistent. His greatest desire is that his accusers and those in judgment over him will become Christians.

---

**1.** What motivates you to tell non-Christians about Jesus?

---

**2.** Read Acts 25:13-27. As is the case with the others who were asked to pronounce judgment on Paul, Festus does not know what to do with Paul. Paul was obviously not guilty or deserving of death or imprisonment. Yet keeping the peace with the Jews was more important to him than justice. Since Festus had already decided what he was going to do with Paul, why do you think he talked to King Agrippa about him?

**3.** Describe the nature and content of Festus' report to Agrippa.

**4.** What is the main point about Christianity that Festus mentions?

**5.** What do you think people most remember about Christianity from your witness?

**6.** Why do you think King Agrippa wanted to hear Paul?

**7.** Read Acts 26. What are the main points about himself that Paul presents in his defense?

**8.** Why does Paul say that he is on trial (26:6-8)?

**9.** How does Paul respond to authority (26:10, 19)?

---

**10.** Contrast the commission of the Sanhedrin (26:9-11) to the commission of Christ (26:15-18).

---

**11.** Describe Paul's final interaction with King Agrippa (26:26-29).

---

**12.** How does Paul's desire for King Agrippa compare or contrast with your desire for those around you who do not know Christ?

---

**13.** How might you move closer to where Paul was in this desire?

**12**

# Paul in Rome!

## *Acts 27—28*

Rome at last!

Paul was innocent. He could have been a free man. But he had appealed to Caesar—and to Caesar he was to go.

As we look at these last two chapters of Acts and complete our study of the life of this marvelous servant of God, it might be worthwhile to ask the questions "Who was really free, and who were the real prisoners?"

---

**1.** What do you think it means to be free?

---

**2.** Read Acts 27—28. Though Paul had every reason by this time to become very self-centered, how do you see him continuing to minister to others throughout these two chapters (27:9-10, 21-25, 31-38, 42-43; 28:3, 8-9, 17-20, 23-31)?

**3.** What do you see of Paul's compassion as he ministers?

How do you need to grow in compassion for others?

---

**4.** What do you think it says about Paul that Julius let him go see his friends (27:3)?

---

**5.** What do you see of Paul's confidence in God throughout this passage?

---

**6.** How were others affected by this great confidence in God?

---

**7.** What are the situations or relationships in your life with non-Christians in which you are tempted to give up on your proclamation of the gospel?

**8.** What truths from this study of Acts encourage you to not give up?

---

**9.** In what other ways would you like your confidence in God to affect those around you?

---

**10.** The words "Boldly and without hindrance he preached the kingdom of God and taught about the Lord Jesus Christ" (28:31) not only summarize Paul's two years in Rome, but his whole Christian life. To what degree would you like this to be a summary of your life? Explain.

---

**11.** In conclusion, what from the book of Acts motivates and equips you to be a witness "to the ends of the earth" (1:8)?

*As we have looked at God's power through his Holy Spirit in the world and in the church may we go forth from Acts, even as Paul did, "boldly and without hindrance proclaiming the kingdom of God and teaching others about the Lord Jesus Christ." Grace and peace be yours.*

## Leader's Notes

Leading a Bible discussion can be an enjoyable and rewarding experience. But it can also be *scary*—especially if you've never done it before. If this is your feeling, you're in good company. When God asked Moses to lead the Israelites out of Egypt, he replied, "O Lord, please send someone else to do it!" (Ex 4:13).

When Solomon became king of Israel, he felt the task was far beyond his abilities. "I am only a little child and do not know how to carry out my duties. . . . Who is able to govern this great people of yours?" (1 Kings 3:7, 9).

When God called Jeremiah to be a prophet, he replied, "Ah, Sovereign LORD, . . . I do not know how to speak; I am only a child" (Jer 1:6).

The list goes on. The apostles were "unschooled, ordinary men" (Acts 4:13). Timothy was young, frail and frightened. Paul's "thorn in the flesh" made him feel weak. But God's response to all of his servants—including you—is essentially the same: "My grace is sufficient for you" (2 Cor 12:9). Relax. God helped these people in spite of their weaknesses, and he can help you in spite of your feelings of inadequacy.

There is another reason why you should feel encouraged. Leading a Bible discussion is not difficult if you follow certain guidelines. You don't need to be an expert on the Bible or a trained teacher. The suggestions listed below should enable you to effectively and enjoyably fulfill your role as leader.

### Preparing to Lead

**1.** Ask God to help you understand and apply the passage to your own life. Unless this happens, you will not be prepared to lead others. Pray too for the various members of the group. Ask God to give you an enjoyable and profitable time together studying his Word.

**2.** As you begin each study, read and reread the assigned Bible passage to familiarize yourself with what the author is saying. In the case of book studies, you may want to read through the entire book prior to the first study. This will give you a helpful overview of its contents.

**3.** This study guide is based on the New International Version of the Bible. It will help you and the group if you use this translation as the basis for your study and discussion. Encourage others to use the NIV also, but allow them the freedom to use whatever translation they prefer.

**4.** Carefully work through each question in the study. Spend time in meditation and reflection as you formulate your answers.

**5.** Write your answers in the space provided in the study guide. This will help you to express your understanding of the passage clearly.

**6.** It might help you to have a Bible dictionary handy. Use it to look up any unfamiliar words, names or places. (For additional help on how to study a passage, see chapter five of *Leading Bible Discussions,* IVP.)

**7.** Once you have finished your own study of the passage, familiarize yourself with the leader's notes for the study you are leading. These are designed to help you in several ways. First, they tell you the purpose the study guide author had in mind while writing the study. Take time to think through how the study questions work together to accomplish that purpose. Second, the notes provide you with additional background information or comments on some of the questions. This information can be useful if people have difficulty understanding or answering a question. Third, the leader's notes can alert you to potential problems you may encounter during the study.

**8.** If you wish to remind yourself of anything mentioned in the leader's notes, make a note to yourself below that question in the study.

**Leading the Study**

**1.** Begin the study on time. Unless you are leading an evangelistic Bible study, open with prayer, asking God to help you to understand and apply the passage.

**2.** Be sure that everyone in your group has a study guide. Encourage them to prepare beforehand for each discussion by working through the questions in the guide.

**3.** At the beginning of your first time together, explain that these studies are meant to be discussions not lectures. Encourage the members of the group to participate. However, do not put pressure on those who may be hesitant to speak during the first few sessions.

**4.** Read the introductory paragraph at the beginning of the discussion. This will orient the group to the passage being studied.

**5.** Read the passage aloud if you are studying one chapter or less. You may choose to do this yourself, or someone else may read if he or she has been asked to do so prior to the study. Longer passages may occasionally be read in parts at different times during the study. Some studies may cover several chapters. In such cases reading aloud would probably take too much time, so the group members should simply read the assigned passages prior to the study.

**6.** As you begin to ask the questions in the guide, keep several things in mind. First, the questions are designed to be used just as they are written. If you wish, you may simply read them aloud to the group. Or you may prefer to express them in your own words. However, unnecessary rewording of the questions is not recommended.

Second, the questions are intended to guide the group toward understanding and applying the *main idea* of the passage. The author of the guide has stated his or her view of this central idea in the *purpose* of the study in the leader's notes. You should try to understand how the passage expresses this idea and how the study questions work together to lead the group in that direction.

There may be times when it is appropriate to deviate from the study guide. For example, a question may have already been answered. If so, move on to the next question. Or someone may raise an important question not covered in the guide. Take time to discuss it! The important thing is to use discretion. There may be many routes you can travel to reach the goal of the study. But the easiest route is usually the one the author has suggested.

**7.** Avoid answering your own questions. If necessary, repeat or rephrase them until they are clearly understood. An eager group quickly becomes passive and silent if they think the leader will do most of the talking.

**8.** Don't be afraid of silence. People may need time to think about the question before formulating their answers.

**9.** Don't be content with just one answer. Ask, "What do the rest of you think?" or "Anything else?" until several people have given answers to the question.

**10.** Acknowledge all contributions. Try to be affirming whenever possible. Never reject an answer. If it is clearly wrong, ask, "Which verse led you to that conclusion?" or again, "What do the rest of you think?"

**11.** Don't expect every answer to be addressed to you, even though this will probably happen at first. As group members become more at ease, they will begin to truly interact with each other. This is one sign of a healthy discussion.

**12.** Don't be afraid of controversy. It can be very stimulating. If you don't resolve an issue completely, don't be frustrated. Move on and keep it in mind for later. A subsequent study may solve the problem.

**13.** Stick to the passage under consideration. It should be the source for answering the questions. Discourage the group from unnecessary cross-referencing. Likewise, stick to the subject and avoid going off on tangents.

**14.** Periodically summarize what the *group* has said about the passage. This helps to draw together the various ideas mentioned and gives continuity to the study. But don't preach.

**15.** Conclude your time together with conversational prayer. Be sure to ask God's help to apply those things which you learned in the study.

**16.** End on time.

Many more suggestions and helps are found in *Leading Bible Discussions* (IVP). Reading and studying through that would be well worth your time.

**Components of Small Groups**

A healthy small group should do more than study the Bible. There are four components you should consider as you structure your time together.

*Nurture.* Being a part of a small group should be a nurturing and edifying experience. You should grow in your knowledge and love of God and each other. If we are to properly love God, we must know and keep his commandments (Jn 14:15). That is why Bible study should be a foundational part of your small group. But you can be nurtured by other things as well. You can memorize Scripture, read and discuss a book, or occasionally listen to a tape of a good speaker.

*Community.* Most people have a need for close friendships. Your small group can be an excellent place to cultivate such relationships. Allow time for informal interaction before and after the study. Have a time of sharing during the meeting. Do fun things together as a group, such as a potluck supper or a picnic. Have someone bring refreshments to the meeting. Be creative!

*Worship.* A portion of your time together can be spent in worship and prayer. Praise God together for who he is. Thank him for what he has done and is doing in your lives and in the world. Pray for each other's needs. Ask God to help you to apply what you have learned. Sing hymns together.

*Mission.* Many small groups decide to work together in some form of outreach. This can be a practical way of applying what you have learned. You can host a series of evangelistic discussions for your friends or neighbors. You can visit people at a home for the elderly. Help a widow with cleaning or repair jobs around her home. Such projects can have a transforming influence on your group.

For a detailed discussion of the nature and function of small groups, read *Small Group Leaders'*

*Handbook* or *Good Things Come in Small Groups* (both from IVP).

**Study 1. You Will Be My Witnesses. Acts 1.**

*Purpose:* To understand the task of the church of Jesus Christ and his promise to equip us for that task.

**Question 1.** Every study begins with an "approach" question, which is meant to be asked before the passage is read. These questions are important for several reasons.

First, they help the group to warm up to each other. No matter how well a group may know each other, there is always a stiffness that needs to be overcome before people will begin to talk openly. A good question will break the ice.

Second, approach questions get people thinking along the lines of the topic of the study. Most people will have lots of different things going on in their minds (dinner, an important meeting coming up, how to get the car fixed) that will have nothing to do with the study. A creative question will get their attention and draw them into the discussion.

Third, approach questions can reveal where our thoughts or feelings need to be transformed by Scripture. That is why it is especially important not to read the passage before the approach question is asked. The passage will tend to color the honest reactions people would otherwise give because they are, of course, supposed to think the way the Bible does. Giving honest responses before they find out what the Bible says may help them see where their thoughts or attitudes need to be changed.

**Question 2.** The book of Acts is a sequel to the Gospel of Luke. The Gospel of Luke is also addressed to Theophilus, whose name means "dear friend who loves God." As it says in verse 1, the book of Acts continues from where Luke left off in his Gospel. There is a lot of content covered in these 11 verses. This question is meant to give the group an understanding and overview of that material, as well as a grasp of the magnitude of all that has taken place.

It is important to look closely at all the evidence that there is in this orderly account. It is written by a professional, a physician, a person who is used to a scientific approach to data. Jesus had shown himself frequently and given *many convincing proofs* that he was alive. Luke is also strong on retelling powerful personal stories which give his account flavor and appeal.

**Question 4.** We are indeed given the task of being Jesus' witnesses throughout the world. The purpose of this question is to "feel" the awesomeness of the task as first presented to the apostles . . . and for that awesomeness to penetrate us as we continue in the task.

**Question 8.** First, as is very understandable, they are described as "looking intently up into the sky as he was going" or "gazing up into Heaven," as the King James Version puts it (v. 10). Then, they somehow move toward a state of normalcy by going back home to Jerusalem, a three-quarter-mile walk. The walk probably helped in giving time to talk and allow all that had just taken place to settle in. Ultimately, their response was to be together and to pray.

**Question 9.** The most important aspect of "being together" was obedience. In verses 4-5 the report was that Jesus told them not to leave Jerusalem but to wait for the gift his Father promised him, the Holy Spirit. Being together also provided the opportunity for fellowship, encouragement and unity. We need one another.

**Question 11.** It would build their confidence greatly to see again that some of these remarkable things that were happening to them were written down many years before they had happened.

David was a very important patriarch. The direction came from the instructions that were in the quoted passage (Ps 69:25; 109:8).

**Study 2. Receiving the Power. Acts 2.**

*Purpose:* To begin to understand the power of the Holy Spirit and his equipping us for the task of being witnesses throughout the world.

In chapter one the promise of the Holy Spirit is made by the risen Lord. The mission for his Church is clearly defined. In chapter two this promise is fulfilled. It is the power of the Holy Spirit that enables the apostles to be "witnesses first in Jerusalem."

**Question 2.** Help the group to use their imaginations and place themselves in the circumstances as much as possible. They need to remember all that had gone on over the past couple of months from the crucifixion to the ascension and the emotional as well as spiritual impact of it all. Those in the crowd undoubtedly had been aware of much of this, are confused and now face more.

**Question 5.** In the two cited verses Peter addresses "Fellow Jews" and "Men of Israel," in spite of the fact that there are people from many places in the crowd, as is stated in verses 9-11. Peter apparently had not yet caught the vision of worldwide evangelization that was presented in 1:8. We will see in later chapters of Acts how Peter's awareness and perspective change.

**Question 6.** Theophilus, by hearing about Peter's sermon through the author Luke was exposed to Scripture being fulfilled (vv. 17-21, 25-28). When we directly see God doing what he says he will do, we are reassured that the object of our faith is true.

**Question 11.** This question is meant to touch at one of the longings of many believers today. It is a concept worth discussing. You might use such follow-up questions as "When have you experienced true fellowship?" or "How accessible is true fellowship to you?" or "Why is it lacking so today?" during this question or question 13.

**Study 3. Healing Power. Acts 3.**

*Purpose:* To deepen our understanding of the power of God by seeing it demonstrated in the healing of the crippled beggar.

**Question 1.** Sometimes "religious" non-Christians are the least open to hearing about Jesus. At other times the fact that they are religious is a sign of their hunger for and openness to the truth. One of my most exciting experiences of introducing people to Jesus through Bible study was in an adult Sunday-school class. In the class were people who came to church, though many of them were not Christians, because of a genuine hunger and openness.

**Question 2.** The Jews observed three times of prayer: nine o'clock in the morning, three o'clock in the afternoon and sunset. At these times God-fearing Jews and devout Gentiles went to the temple to pray. It would be an ideal place to find those who were open to the truth about Jesus.

"The continued loyalty of the converted Jews to the temple services was mentioned in 2.46; here, then, are Peter and John proceeding thither and finding occasion for action and word in the name of Jesus (6)" (R. V. G. Tasker, gen. ed., *The Acts of the Apostles,* Tyndale New Testament Commentaries [Grand Rapids, Mich.: Eerdmans], p. 62).

**Question 4.** The beggar immediately began praising God. The crowd on the other hand suspected that Peter and John might have been directly responsible for this miracle. Peter was on guard and quickly addressed this matter and drew their attention to Jesus.

**Question 5.** "In charging them Peter echoes the contrasts woven into the Isaiah prophecies. God glorified His Servant; the Jews betrayed Him (13). Pilate acquitted Him; the Jews denied Him (13). He was the Holy One and the Just; the Jews chose a murderer (14). The Jews killed Him; God raised Him from the dead (15)" *(The Acts,* pp. 63-64).

**Question 7.** "Complete healing" suggests spiritual and emotional healing as well as physical healing.

**Question 8.** "After the manner of his first sermon, Peter turns, at verse 17, from stern denunciation to appeal. Let them repent, for their vast evil has not frustrated God. Christ's passion was in God's purpose. Verse 18 should be translated 'His Christ' and that is 'His anointed'. It is a quotation from Ps.11.2, which Peter uses again in fuller form in iv. 26. Christ is still the living and the coming Savior, as the resurrection shows (19-21). Peter's main concern is to remove the Jews' stumbling block. The first and most necessary step in this Jewish evangel was to prove from the testimony of the prophets that the sufferings of the Messiah were part of God's plan. The argument from verses 19-25 may sound to western ears a trifle remote, but it would be illuminating and cogent to minds trained in the thought-forms and language of the Old Testament" *(The Acts,* pp. 63-64).

**Questions 10 and 12.** Help the group to personalize this passage by sharing from their own experiences times of people being open to the truth about Jesus and how the power of God is demonstrated in their lives. It would be very helpful if you begin by sharing from your own experience as a leader.

**Question 11.** The power of the Holy Spirit is demonstrated as the truth about Jesus is proclaimed by the apostles. In verses 1-10 before the man is healed (through the power of the Holy Spirit), the truth about the source of the gift, and that it was a gift better than money, is proclaimed. In verses 11-13 again the source of the power is identified. If the apostles had lied and taken credit for it, the power would not have been demonstrated.

Throughout the rest of the chapter, the truth about Jesus is proclaimed, and the power of the Holy Spirit is demonstrated throughout the book of Acts.

**Study 4. Called into Question. Acts 4:1-31.**

*Purpose:* To understand how the power of God equips us to be his witnesses throughout the world in the midst of both the task and the power being challenged.

**Question 3.** "The apostles are technically on their defence, but actually they have gone over to the attack; Peter proceeds to preach the gospel to his judges, and he does so by citing a well-known OT scripture. 'The stone which the builders rejected has become the head of the corner' (Psalm 118:22) is one of the earliest messianic testimonies. It was so used (by implication) by Jesus Himself, as the conclusion of the Parable of the Vineyard (Mark 12:10). In the original OT context the rejected stone is perhaps Israel, despised by the nations but chosen by God for the accomplishment of His purpose. But, as in so many other instances, the purpose of God for Israel finds its fulfillment in the single-handed work of Christ. So Jesus regards this passage from the Psalter 'as reaching its true fulfillment in Himself, and as prophetic of His own triumph, which will follow His rejection.' This verse from Ps. 118 became one of the passages most frequently quoted by the early Christian teachers to describe the temporary humiliation and subsequent rejection of Jesus the crucified and risen Messiah" (F. F. Bruce, gen. ed., *The Book of Acts,* The

New International Commentary on the New Testament [Grand Rapids, Mich.: Eerdmans, 1974], pp. 99-100).

"Peter, bold as ever, pressed home his accusation where it most properly belonged, warning the supreme court that the same name by which the cripple had received bodily health was the *only* name through which they could receive from God spiritual health. This boldness was the more surprising on the part of 'laymen,' untrained in the rabbinical schools; but these men had been disciples of no ordinary teacher, who had Himself excited the surprised comment: 'How is it that this man has learning, when he has never studied?' (Jn. 7:15)" *(The New Bible Commentary: Revised* [Downers Grove, Ill.: InterVarsity Press, 1970], pp. 977).

**Question 5.** They saw the courage and boldness of Peter and John in proclaiming the gospel. The fact that they were "unlearned men" added to the potency of their stand. They probably remembered the same quality of Jesus' teaching just weeks prior, and they noticed the influence of Jesus on them—"they took note that these men had been with Jesus." It was also hard to stop them because they refused to obey people instead of God.

The evidence of what they claimed stood in their midst in the form of the healed man. Everyone in Jerusalem knew they had done an outstanding miracle that the religious leaders could not deny. The man who was miraculously healed was over forty years old, an age at which such cures just simply do not occur. All the people were praising God, and the religious leaders were afraid of them.

"This," says a Jewish scholar, "was the first mistake which the Jewish leaders made with regard to the new sect. And this mistake was fatal. There was probably no need to arrest the Nazarenes, thus calling attention to them and making them 'martyrs.' But once arrested, they should not have been freed so quickly. The arrest and release increased the number of believers; for these events showed on the one hand that the new sect was a power which the authorities feared enough to persecute, and on the other hand they proved that there was no danger in being a disciple of Jesus (he, of course, being the one who had saved them from the hand of their persecutors!)" (J. Klausner, *From Jesus to Paul* [Eng. tr. London, 1944], pp. 282 ff.).

In summary, there was boldness in proclamation of the truth, even by *unlearned* men. There was the fact that the disciples "had been with Jesus." There was the undeniable evidence of the truth of their message, a healed man, a life that was changed. There was the commitment of obedience to God rather than people, and the fact that what they did and taught was in the name of Jesus.

**Question 6.** Help the group to look carefully at the responses to question 5 and then to discuss this question thoroughly.

**Question 9.** Graciously, God has given us the body of believers as a resource to witness to the world and a place to demonstrate the power of the Holy Spirit. His desire for his body is that they would be one. That oneness, that unity allows for his power to flow freely.

**Question 10.** You may want to encourage the group to explore the definition of "sovereign": "Above or superior to all others; chief, greatest, supreme. Supreme in power, rank or authority. Holding the position of reigning. A person who possesses supreme authority" (Webster's New World Dictionary).

"The two apostles, on their release, returned to the place where the other apostles were, and when they reported their experience before the Sanhedrin, the whole company resorted to prayer.

They addressed God as Sovereign Lord, the Creator of all, in time-honoured language derived from Hebrew scripture" *(The Book of Acts,* pp. 105-6).

**Question 11.** "In these words of the apostles we have an explicit identification of God's 'holy Servant Jesus' with the royal Son of God addressed in Ps. 2:7. Jesus is both the obedient Servant and the one whom God anointed or made Messiah—at His baptism" *(The Book of Acts,* p. 106).

**Question 12.** "The Sanhedrin might threaten, but their threats called not for fear and silence but for increased boldness of speech. The apostles therefore prayed that they themselves might have courage to proclaim their message without fear or favour, and that God would place the seal of His public approval on their witness by granting further mighty works of healing and similar signs and wonders through the same name which had cured the lame man—the name of His 'holy Servant Jesus' " *(The Book of Acts,* pp. 106-7).

**Study 5. Oneness of Heart. Acts 4:32—5:16.**

*Purpose:* To observe the unity of the church as an expression of the power of the Holy Spirit.

**Question 2.** "The spirit-filled community exhibited a remarkable unanimity, which expressed itself even in the attitude to private property. Each member regarded his private estate as being at the community's disposal: those who possessed houses and lands sold them in order that they might be more conveniently available to the community in the form of money. The richer members thus made provision for the poorer, and for a time no one had any room to complain of hunger and want. The apostles, as the community leaders, received the free-will offerings that were brought, but they apparently delegated the details of distribution to others, for they themselves had to devote their time and energy to their public testimony to the risen Christ. As they did so, the power of God shown in mighty works, attended their preaching the very thing for which they had prayed (vs. 30). And they continued to enjoy the grace of God and the Jerusalem populace" *(The Book of Acts,* pp. 108-9).

**Question 5.** This is a speculative question. Allow the group to brainstorm and investigate how they might feel if they observed such an incident.

**Question 6.** "The sovereign presence of the Holy Spirit is so real that any action done to the church is regarded as done to the Spirit, just as any action taken by the church is predicated of the Spirit" *(The New Bible Commentary,* pp. 978).

This narrative emphasizes the Spirit's indwelling presence in the church and the practical and solemn implications of that.

**Question 7.** Be sure to give this question the time it needs to help the group evaluate how "lying" takes place. It is an important issue and can be subtle. We can lie by speaking half-truths, by sharing information about others that we do not know is truth (not that knowing it is true automatically makes it all right to share), pretending that we are something that we are not, refusing to admit failure or confess sin, and so on.

**Question 8.** Truth and integrity are basic to trust and without trust a community withers and dies.

**Question 10.** They probably feared the kind of persecution the apostles were facing.

**Study 6. Persecution and Expansion. Acts 5:17—6:7.**

*Purpose:* To consider the total inadequacy of those who attempted to thwart the growth of the church of Jesus Christ through opposition and persecution and to observe how the church continued to expand.

**Question 2.** This is an overview question. It is to help your group get a grasp of the events of this passage. Move the group through the passage without getting bogged down with details. Do, however, consider the more covert episodes of emotion as well as the more obvious. For example, after discussing the more obvious, ask such follow-up questions as: How do you think the apostles felt as the angel "opened the doors of the jail and brought them out" (v. 19)? What might the officers have felt when they arrived at the jail and found the apostles gone (v. 22)?

**Question 4.** What happened to the apostles is dramatic. This kind of dramatic situation is not necessary for members of your group to respond to this question and to apply what we are learning to their lives and churches. Some questions that might help are: What situations in your life are calling for difficult, consistent obedience? In what situations of proclaiming the gospel do you need the peace of the Holy Spirit, perseverance? Are there relationships in your life in which clear proclamation of the good news of Jesus is needed, even if it is rejected? What decisions do you need to make to obey God rather than follow a cultural norm?

**Question 6.** His message was, "God is over all. Let these men go, and we will see if they are of God." It strikes me that the fact that Gamaliel's words—the words of an unbeliever—were used to persuade them to spare the apostles' lives is an example of "God's being over all."

**Question 9.** They listened to the needs of the people and they acted. They delegated the work. They gave criteria for choosing the men. They recognized the spiritual nature of the work of the seven and laid their hands on them. The Twelve did not try to do it all themselves. They knew their call was to give attention to the ministry of the Word and prayer.

**Study 7. Stephen, Full of Spirit and Wisdom. Acts 6:8—7:60.**

*Purpose:* To consider God's Spirit and wisdom in Stephen and to seek to make them more a part of our lives.

**Question 1.** As you prepare to lead your group through this passage, ask God to work in the group for them to desire to be filled with the Holy Spirit and his wisdom.

**Question 2.** Allow a few minutes for the group to scan the passage and get to know Stephen. You might ask such follow-up questions as: What does it mean to be "full of grace and power" (v. 8)? What do you think was significant about "his face being like the face of an angel"? What impact would this have on the crowd? Describe the way that he proclaimed truth (vv. 51-53). What were his character and spirit like (vv. 59-60)?

You certainly do not want to use all these questions. You may not need any of them. It depends how well your group gets into knowing and experiencing Stephen on their own and how much help they need.

**Question 3.** Stephen reminds us of Jesus. Throughout the gospels, people are amazed at the wisdom and authority Jesus spoke with.

> Stephen expounded the implications of Jesus' Messiahship more radically than his fellow-believers had hitherto expounded it. The strength of his case was such that his opponents in the debate found themselves worsted. They accepted his premises (which were based on their joint acknowledgment of the authority of OT Scripture, but they refused to accept his

> conclusions, so scandalous and revolutionary did they appear. (F. F. Bruce, *The Book of Acts,* pp. 133-34)

**Question 4.** It seems that Stephen had a greater comprehension of a more spiritual worship that entered with Christianity and which did not depend on the ceremonial law or the temple. This is why the charges were brought against him. He was more farsighted than the other leaders in Christianity in his comprehension of the breach with Judaic worship that Christianity brought with it. In this he blazed the trail for Paul and the writer of Hebrews.

> The Twelve had kept the respect and goodwill of the Jerusalem populace; they attended the Temple services regularly, and appeared outwardly to be observant Jews whose only distinction from others was that they believed and proclaimed Jesus to be the Messiah. But a new note was heard in the debates in the Hellenistic synagogue which Stephen attended, a note which envisaged the abolition of the Temple cultus and the institution of a new and more spiritual form of worship. If the charges made by Stephen's accusers are garbled, yet we are not at a loss to discover the real trend of his arguments.
>
> His speech is a reasoned exposition of his teaching about the transitory nature of the Jewish worship. An attack on the temple, as Stephen's teaching was construed to be, ranked as blasphemy of the worst kind; there was also the subordinate consideration that the economy of Jerusalem was based on the temple. The rulers at once saw their opportunity, and arraigned Stephen on a poppular charge. *(The New Bible,* p. 979)

**Question 5.** Stephen's defense is a review of the history of Israel. It takes the form of a historical retrospect—a form well established in Jewish tradition. He introduces the content of his response to the accusations; the building of Solomon's temple and the giving of the law on Mt. Sinai. The refusal of their forefathers to obey Moses, the fact that their forefathers had the tabernacle in the desert and were able to worship there, and the fact that God cannot be maintained in a particular place are other important points.

**Questions 11-12.** Make sure there is time to discuss these questions and that they are not just tacked on. Also, allow time to pray about what is learned.

**Study 8. The Power of Suffering. Acts 8:1-40.**

*Purpose:* To observe the expansion of the church in the midst of persecution and suffering and to integrate into our lives the principles of evangelism that are observed in this process.

**Question 2.** "The persecution and dispersion, however, brought about a beginning of the fulfillment of our Lord's commission to His disciples in Ch. 1:8, 'ye shall be my witnesses both in Jerusalem, and in all Judaea and Samaria. . . .' 'The churches of God which are in Judaea in Christ Jesus' (to borrow Paul's language in 1 Thes. 2:14) were born in this time of persecution" (F. F. Bruce, *The Book of Acts,* p. 175).

Because of the disdain of the Jews for the Samaritans, it was a bold act on Philip's part to proclaim the good news to the Samaritans. The Samaritans did however share with many of the Jews the hope of the coming Messiah.

"Peter and John were sent to Samaria to find out whether or not the Samaritans were truly becoming believers. The Jewish Christians, even the apostles, were still unsure whether Gentiles (non-Jews) and half Jews could receive the Holy Spirit. It wasn't until Peter's experience with Cornelius (chapter 10) the apostles became fully convinced that the Holy Spirit was for all people" *(The Life Application Bible* [Wheaton, Ill.: Tyndale House], pp. 1636).

**Question 3.** Do not overlook the work that the Spirit did in Philip in a more quiet way as well as the more dramatic acts of the Spirit of God.

**Question 5.** The way to receive God's power is to ask God's forgiveness, turn from sin and receive the Holy Spirit. God's power comes from repentance and belief in Christ as Savior. This is quite opposite to the world's view of receiving power.

**Question 6.** There is some debate as to the authenticity of Simon's conversion. Help the group to not spend too much time in this type of debate but rather move more deeply through the principles discussed here.

> Philip appears to have accepted this man's discipleship, and indeed his professed adherence to the Church may have been set down as a remarkable conversion. . . . His faith was concerned with miracles (13, 19, 20), and ended in amazement, not holiness; his view of God was materialistic; his aim was self-aggrandizement; he was afraid, but not visibly repentant. (R. V. G. Tasker, *The Acts,* p. 73)

This is where he began. Whether his conversion was real or not, the principles of discipleship and confrontation are important. Redemption is a process, and Simon had much to be redeemed from his old life, assuming the conversion was real.

**Question 8.** "Ethiopia was located in Africa south of Egypt. The eunuch was obviously very dedicated to God because he came such a long distance to worship in Jerusalem. The Jews had contact with Ethiopia in ancient days (Psalms 63:31; Jeremiah 38:7), so this man may have been a Gentile convert to Judaism. Because he was the treasurer of Ethiopia, his conversion brought Christianity into the power structures of another government. This is the beginning of the witness 'to the ends of the earth' (1:8). Isaiah had prophesied that Gentiles and eunuchs would be blessed (Isaiah 56:3-5)" *(The Life Application Bible,* p. 1636).

**Question 9.** Have the group scan back through the passage to look for the kinds of evangelism. This question is not as important as the next. The purpose of the question is to observe the fact that God certainly works in all kinds of ways and all types of situations. It also is to encourage your group members to think through how they most effectively can communicate the gospel.

**Question 10.** Cover this question thoroughly. Remember such things as the vital, indispensable role of the Holy Spirit in conversion and in leading you to opportunities where people are ready. Obedience to his voice is vital. Also, the place of the Word is important in communicating the faith. And there is much more.

**Study 9. Saul's Conversion. Acts 9:1-31.**

*Purpose:* To consider God's miraculous work in Saul's conversion and the effect of this on the whole church.

**Question 2.** "The narrative now returns to Saul of Tarsus and his campaign of repression against the Christians, which received brief mention in 8:3. He was not content with driving them from Jerusalem; they must be pursued and rooted out wherever they fled, not only within the frontiers of the land of Israel but beyond them as well. 'In raging fury against them'—to quote his own words at a later time—'I persecuted them even to foreign cities' (Ch. 26:11, RSV)" (F. F. Bruce, *The Book of Acts,* p. 193).

The high priest was in charge of the internal affairs of the Jewish state. His authority was upheld by the Roman power. His decrees were binding to a great degree in Jewish communities outside Palestine.

Someone in the group may have a question about the use of the phrase "the Way." "The name by which Christianity here is described, 'The Way' (v 2) recurs in Chs. 19:9, 23; 22:4; 24:14, 22. That was evidently a term used by the early Christians to denote their own movement, considered as the way of life or the way of salvation" (F. F. Bruce, *The Book of Acts,* p. 194).

**Question 3.** Paul himself gave one consistent account of this encounter with Christ. In that one illuminating flash he saw the glorified Christ and in the voice that followed he heard Christ speak.

"The more one studies the event, the more one agrees with the eighteenth century English statesman, George Lyttelton, that 'the conversion and apostleship of St. Paul alone, duly considered, was of itself a demonstration sufficient to prove Christianity to be a divine revelation' " (F. F. Bruce, *The Book of Acts,* p. 196).

**Question 4.** Help the group to look carefully at these two encounters with the Lord. Comparison and contrast are effective ways of doing this.

Examples of the contrasts include: Saul asking, "Who are you, Lord?" while Ananias knew immediately who was calling him. The Lord asks Saul a question about Saul's response to him, but with Ananias the relationship is established, and he begins with instructions.

Examples of how the two encounters compare are: Both respond with obedience. And questions were allowed and responded to by the Lord. Look carefully for others.

**Question 5.** It is especially hard to show love to those we fear or whose motives we doubt. Ananias was both afraid of and doubted Saul. Out of obedience to the Lord, he greeted Saul lovingly, even as a brother. He was accepted as one of the family of God.

**Question 10.** You might want to help your group think through what might have happened if Barnabas had not defended Saul to the believers who were afraid of him.

**Question 11.** Barnabas was one of the Jewish converts mentioned in 4:36. He became the bridge between Saul and the other Christians and apostles.

New Christians need help and support. They need people more experienced in the faith who will walk with them, teach, encourage and introduce them to other believers. Help the group to think through how this has happened to them and specifically how they can become this to young believers that they lead to the Lord or know. They should discuss how they would like to grow in this area and even set some goals.

**Study 10. Salvation for Every Nation. Acts 9:32—10:48.**

*Purpose:* To increase our understanding of the potential of the gospel to reach every person in all the corners of the world.

**Question 3.** Having been used of God to raise someone from the dead might make the impossibility of taking the gospel to the Gentiles more "possible."

**Question 7.** In verse 14 Peter questions God. This happens three times. Peter wonders about the vision. In spite of uncertainty Peter invited the Gentiles into his home and went with them the next day. In verse 28 Peter reminds Cornelius that it is against the Jewish law for him to associate with a Gentile. He shares what God has shown him from the vision. (He still seems skeptical.) Cornelius' explanation seems to increase Peter's understanding and he says, "I now realize *how true* it is that God does not show favoritism but accepts men from every nation who fear him and do what is right." Peter was then willing to share the message with the Gentiles, observe and acknowledge the outpouring of the Spirit upon them and even initiate their being baptized (baptism constitutes their entry into the Christian church).

**Question 8.** Cornelius was expecting them, invited friends and relatives in and received Peter with great respect.

**Question 9.** Lessons we can learn from the story of Cornelius include: God reaches those who want to know him. The gospel is for all people. There are people who are eager to believe everywhere.

**Question 10.** See 10:9-48. Trace carefully all that God does for Peter in this process of taking the gospel to the Gentiles.

**Question 12.** Not only was the gospel spread to Gentiles and the first Gentile church established, but Cornelius was responsible for one hundred soldiers and would probably be returning to Rome soon. His conversion was a major stepping-stone for spreading the gospel to the capital city.

**Study 11. The First Jewish-Gentile Church. Acts 11.**

*Purpose:* To observe how the church is progressing from a Jewish church separate from the Gentiles to a Jewish-Gentile fellowship.

**Question 4.** Peter is matter of fact and not defensive. He shared all the details and told them precisely how it happened. He was honest and vulnerable about his own questions and doubts. And he shared his deep conviction about what God had done—"So if God gave them the same gift as he gave us, who believed in the Lord Jesus Christ, who was I to think that I could oppose God?"

**Question 7.** The early church was very conscientious about nurturing their new believers. In this passage Barnabas is sent up to Antioch when news reached the church in Jerusalem that people were turning to the Lord. As he saw what needed to be done, he got more help. He went after Saul in Tarsus. They met with the church at Antioch for a whole year.

**Question 8.** In verses 22-26 Barnabas is described as sensitive to, and glad for, God's grace and work. He was encouraging and full of the Holy Spirit and faith. He was persistent and thorough.

> The leaders of the Jerusalem church recognized the novelty of the situation at Antioch when news of it reached them, and just as Peter and John had earlier gone to Samaria to investigate Philip's missionary service there, so now Jerusalem sent a delegate to Antioch to look into the strange events that were being enacted in that great city. It was a critical moment; much—far more than they could have realized—depended on the delegate whom they chose to send. In the providence of God, they chose the best man for this delicate and important work—Barnabas, the "son of encouragement." Barnabas himself was a Cypriote Jew by birth, like some of those who had begun to preach the gospel to the Antiochene Gentiles, and his sympathies would in any case be wider than those of Jewish Christians who had never set foot outside Judaea. (F. F. Bruce, *The Book of Acts,* p. 240)

**Question 11.** To be sure, we have the same biases as the early Jewish church had. We just have different starting points. Help your group discuss these in light of what our Christian response should be.

**Study 12. Miraculous Escape. Acts 12.**

*Purpose:* To deepen our understanding of the power of God as we see it demonstrated in the escape of Peter from prison, by Herod's death and in the increase and spread of the Word of God even in the midst of great opposition.

**Question 2.** Help the group to look carefully at the people and to notice little details like: Peter is sleeping soundly in prison, but Herod has four men at a time guarding him. (Notice Peter's peace in comparison to Herod's fear and apprehension.)

**Question 3.** "During his brief reign over Judea (41-44), Herod, despite his faults, proved a studious patron of the Jewish faith, and maintained friendly relations with the religious leaders of the people. It is said that on one occasion, when reading the law at the Feast of Tabernacles, he burst into tears as he read Dt. 17:15 ('one from among your brethren you shall set as king over you; you may not put a foreigner over you, who is not your brother'), for he remembered the Edomite origin of the Herod family; but the populace cried out: 'Be not distressed; you are our brother!' " *(The New Bible,* p. 987).

"His execution of James the Zebedean, and his arrest of Peter, are related here. The words, 'he saw that it pleased the Jews,' are significant, for reasons already suggested" *(The New Bible,* p. 987).

> Herod's attack on the church was no doubt a policy move to gratify and conciliate the old Pharisaic and Sadducean enemies of the Church.
>
> The persecution, therefore, and the imprisonment of Peter recorded in this chapter, follow in direct sequence the events narrated in X. I-XI 18. The zealous observance, which had heretofore marked the Jerusalem church, had gone far to allay the fears of the religious leaders.
>
> Provided Christianity remained within the strict Jewish fold, and confined its activities to the framework of the old faith, the Sadducees had no fault to find with it, and the Pharisees found no cause for complaint. But Peter's report caused alarm which spread beyond the confines of the Church. Vested interests took fright, and, either directly persuaded, or sensing an opportunity, the king started this petty persecution." (R. V. G. Tasker, *The Acts,* p. 99)

**Question 5.** "Peter was in the custody of four soldiers at a time, of whom two were probably on guard at either side of him and two at the door" *(The New Bible,* p. 987).

**Question 7.** There are times that God does unusual things or answers prayers in dramatic ways and allows us to see them. The response of others to this could be, in so many words, "You are out of your mind," that is, "That can't be." When has this happened to you?

**Question 9.** "The persecutor dies; the cause he persecuted survives in increasing vigor" *(The New Bible,* p. 988).

**Question 11.** As the leader, be sure to prepare a list of the things you see throughout the first twelve chapters. Help the group to move through this review and discuss what they have learned.

**Part 2. God's Power at the Ends of the Earth. Acts 13—28.**

**Study 1. Paul's First Missionary Journey. Acts 13—14.**

*Purpose:* To examine Paul's personal qualities that made him effective in the task of worldwide evangelization.

**Question 2.** The leaders of the church were united and established an atmosphere of worship, prayer and fasting in which they could be sensitive to God's voice and purpose for those in their fellowship. They were obedient to God and placed hands on Saul and Barnabas and sent them off, supported and prayed for.

> There are indications that NT Christians were especially sensitive to the Spirit's communications during fasting. On this occasion the divine message directed the leaders of the church to set Barnabas and Saul apart for a special work to which He had called them. It is perhaps worth noticing that the two men who were to be released for what we nowadays call missionary service overseas were the two most eminent and gifted leaders in the church. (F. F. Bruce, *The Book of Acts,* p. 261)

The world ministry which thus began was destined to change the history of Europe and the world.

It is important to recognize and practice what was done in relationship to Saul and Barnabas' call to this ministry as we consider being called by God to worldwide evangelization. It was in the context of Christian community that they were called and sent out. We can assume that this prayer support for them continued throughout the three years that they were gone. They also were the community to whom Saul and Barnabas were accountable and reported back to.

**Question 4.** "The history of the Jewish people, Paul maintains, becomes intelligible only in the consummation found in Christ, in whom the promise, given originally to the Jews, found fulfillment. The Law cannot save; it is incomplete (27, 32, 33, 39). This, of course, is the theme of the Epistle to the Galatians. In spite of God's preparation through all history (17-23), and especially through the ministry of the Forerunner (24, 25), the Jews of Jerusalem rejected Him (27-29), but in so doing fulfilled prophecy, and set atonement and resurrection in the gospel (30-41)" (R. V. G. Tasker, *The Acts,* p. 105).

**Question 11.** As you lead the group in responding to this question, consider such aspects as starting in the Jewish synagogues on the sabbath, being led by the Holy Spirit, clearly presenting truth, using Scripture as the basis of all that they said, and going where people were open to what they had to say. Also consider the towns they travelled to, the crosscultural emphasis, and the emphasis placed on choosing, encouraging and training leaders. They confronted opposition and evil head on (13:9-11).

"The practice of announcing the Christian message first of all in the Jewish synagogue or synagogues of each city they visited was to be a regular feature of Barnabas and Paul's missionary procedure. It was a practical expression of the principle that Paul lays down in Rom. 1:16—that the gospel is to be presented 'to the Jew first.' Besides, Paul 'was always sure of a good opening for his Gentile mission among the "God-fearing," who formed part of his audience in every synagogue' " (F. F. Bruce, *The Book of Acts,* p. 263).

They were *sent from* Antioch which was an important city to the Roman Empire. It was the cosmopolitan meeting-place of Jew, Greek, Roman and Syrian. Here Christianity first encountered the full broad stream of the Empire's varied life. Here the faith first attracted pagan attention. "You will be my witnesses in Jerusalem, and in all Judea and Samaria, and to the ends of the earth" (Acts 1:8).

They *traveled to* main towns where lots of people were and where people traveled in and out of. Cyprus was an island of great importance in the Near East from early times.

Finally, do not overlook the process in which Barnabas moves from the driver's seat to the back seat. When the expedition sets out from Syria, the order is "Barnabas and Saul"; by the time they leave Cyprus, it is "Paul and his company"!

"Barnabas does not seem to have resented this at all: his greatness of soul illustrates the old couplet—

'It takes more grace than I can tell
To play the second fiddle well.' "

(F. F. Bruce, *The Book of Acts,* p. 266)

**Study 2. Conflict in the Church. Acts 15.**

*Purpose:* To consider ways of handling conflict within the Christian community.

**Question 2.** Set the stage for this drama. Who is there? What are the circumstances of this conflict?

**Questions 3-4.** Look carefully and help the group to respond fully to this question. Conflict within the Christian community is a great enemy within the church today because it is often not dealt with biblically. The response to this question is the base for question 5, observing principles that are vital in conflict resolution today and question 6—where do I need help?

The first step was acknowledging that there was conflict. It was not glossed over. There was an open spirit to deal with the conflict. They sent people up to Jerusalem, where the conflict began.

They focused on God, rather than on the conflict. As Paul and Barnabas went up to Jerusalem, they told people of all the wonderful works of God. That was what they started with when arriving in Jerusalem.

The believers in Jerusalem "welcomed" them. They did not begrudge their coming. There was no reserve or resentment. They were all open to listening to each other as well as sharing their perspective in a loving way. They spoke from their experience of seeing God work among the Gentiles and they spoke from the Word of God. They realized the necessity that the Word and their experience were in agreement.

Their desire as a body was to encourage the new Gentile converts. They loved them. They responded to them and directed them. They spoke openly of their brotherhood with the Gentile believers. They did not lord seniority or position over them. They demonstrated the importance of the new believers by sending people to encourage them and to communicate with them as well as a letter.

The new believers were encouraged. They then separated in peace. They hadn't forced on the new Christians a pattern of behavior that was non-essential to being a Christian.

**Question 7.** They were each deeply dedicated to the service of Christ. They were as one in their determination to take God's love to the world and in doctrinal belief. They agreed that it was a good idea to visit the churches they had planted and even that they needed another team member. Their history which we have observed up to this point would speak of a strong base of relationship and unity.

**Question 9.** Finding a temporary solution is better than continued warfare. It allowed them to continue to serve the Lord. There were two teams that went out instead of one. It gave time for the two of them to more thoroughly seek God's mind for a solution.

We have reason to believe from Scripture that Paul and Barnabas were reconciled (2 Tim 4:11;

1 Cor 9:6; Gal 2:11-13). Their not-so-perfect short-term solution made it possible for healing in the long run.

**Question 11.** We are short-sighted human beings. Though we certainly should have strong convictions and be able to communicate those to others, the way we do that communicating is very important. Horace Fenton, Jr., in his book *When Christians Clash* (Downers Grove, Ill.: InterVarsity Press, 1987) speaks of "advancing our arguments against fellow Christians with what one wise man paradoxically called 'tentative finality.' " The fact that Paul and Barnabas did not have a full picture should not have silenced them, but it should have reminded them of their fallibility.

**Study 3. What Must I Do? Acts 16.**

*Purpose:* To understand the significance of immediate and unreserved obedience to the call of God.

**Background.** "It was Timothy's mixed parentage that made Paul decide to circumcise him before taking him along as a travel-companion. In the eyes of Jews, Timothy was a Gentile because he was the uncircumcised son of a Greek. In Gentile eyes, however, he was practically a Jew, having been brought up in his mother's religion. Paul therefore regularized his status (and in Jewish eyes, legitimized him) by circumcising him" (F. F. Bruce, *The Book of Acts,* p. 322).

Timothy was not required to be circumcised. The council at Jerusalem had already decided this. But he voluntarily did this to overcome any barriers to his witness for Christ.

Help your group to think through what it means to be guided by God. It is important to be willing at any time to lay aside our own plans, as good and well intentioned as they may be, in response to the Spirit's prompting. Though Paul had a thoughtful plan of action and travel, he changed those without apparent question when told by the Spirit on two different occasions not to go or to preach somewhere. Other principles of guidance are: ask God to open and close doors of circumstances to lead you; pray continually about plans and direction; talk with mature, godly Christians; check out your internal motivation for taking such actions, and make sure your plan is true to the principles in God's Word. And, finally, be ready for God to speak to you in whatever way he chooses. He will lead both in the direction that he wants us to take, but also away from the wrong direction or situation.

**Question 6.** Opposition to the truth of the gospel today can be very overt or quite subtle. It can come from both Christians and non-Christians—very subtly when from Christians. It can take the form of physical, emotional and spiritual persecution. The reasons can be such things as material gain, social status, threat to other religions and dogma, or fear of what response and obedience to the gospel might mean in one's life.

**Question 7.** Lead the group in looking carefully at the whole story of the conversion of the Philippian jailor. Discuss all the details that could have influenced the jailor to come to the Lord from the attitudes of Paul and Silas, to the earthquake, to the miracle of all the prisoners still being present. Examine all the possible ways that God chose to work in this situation.

**Question 10.** "Three individuals are singled out by Luke among Paul's converts at Philippi, and they differ so much one from another that he might be thought to have deliberately selected them in order to show how the saving name of Jesus proved its power in the lives of the most diverse types of men and women. The first is Lydia, the independent business-woman of reputable character and God-fearing mind; as she heard the gospel story, 'the Lord opened her heart to give heed to what was said by Paul' (RSV). But the second is a person of a very different stamp: an unfortunate demon-possessed slave-girl, whose owners exploited her infirmity for their material profit. She is described by Luke as a 'pythoness', *i.e.* as a person inspired by Apollo, the god particularly associated with the giving of oracles, who was worshipped as the 'Pythian' god at the oracular shrine of Delphi (otherwise called Pytho) in central Greece. Her involuntary utterances were regarded as the voice of the god, and she was thus much in demand by people who wished to have their fortunes told.

"Her deliverance demanded much more spectacular measures than did Lydia's quiet turning in heart to the Lord. Day by day, as the missionaries went to the place of prayer, she followed them through the streets of Philippi, advertising them aloud as servants of the Most High God, who proclaimed the way of salvation. The title, 'Most High God,' was one which provided Jews and Gentiles with a convenient common denominator for the Supreme Being, and 'salvation' in the religious sense was as eagerly sought by Gentiles as by Jews.

"The missionaries, however, did not appreciate her 'unsolicited testimonials', and at last Paul, vexed by her continual clamour, exorcized the spirit that possessed her, commanding it in the name of Jesus Christ to come out of her. The words had scarcely left his lips before she was released from her familiar spirit" (F. F. Bruce, *The Book of Acts,* pp. 332-33).

The final convert, quite different from both of the women, was a jailor who embraced the message of salvation with joy. The gospel was affecting all levels of society.

**Study 4. An Unknown God. Acts 17.**

*Purpose:* To observe how Paul understands and responds to the different cultures to whom he is communicating the gospel and to be motivated to understand the people and culture of those to whom God has called us to minister.

**Question 1.** This is a good time to look at the modern-day philosophies that are thriving in our world. Consider such things as the New Age, Eastern mysticism, Satan worship, the occult world, humanism, liberalism and others.

**Question 2.** Question two is an overview to lead the group to look over the whole passage.

> In accordance with his regular practice, (in Thessalonica) Paul visited the local synagogue, and (having probably been asked to speak, as previously at Pisidian Antioch) he expounded the OT scriptures on three successive sabbath days, bringing forward as evidence of their fulfillment the historic facts accomplished in the ministry, death and exaltation of Jesus, setting the fulfillment alongside the predictions in order that the force of his argument might be readily grasped. According to these predictions, the Messiah was appointed to suffer and then to rise from the dead; both these experiences had been fulfilled in Jesus of Nazareth (and in nobody else); therefore, said he, "this is the Messiah, this Jesus whom I am proclaiming to you." (F. F. Bruce, *The Book of Acts,* p. 343)

In Thessalonica some Jews believed and more God-fearing Greeks believed. Some of the Jews who did not believe were incensed and began rioting against Paul and his companions. They were accused of revolutionary activity against the Roman Empire.

"The apostles proclaimed the kingdom of God, a very different kingdom from any secular empire, and no doubt they gave Jesus the Greek title basileus ("king"), by which the Roman

Emperor was described by his Greekspeaking subjects" (F. F. Bruce, *The Book of Acts*, p. 345).

In Berea Paul again began in the synagogue, but the reception given by the Jewish community was far different than that in Thessalonica.

> For, with commendable open-mindedness, they brought the claims made by Paul to the touchstone of Holy Writ instead of giving way to prejudice. Their procedure, "examining the scriptures daily to see if these things were so" (RSV), is worthy of imitation by all who have some new form of religious teaching pressed upon their acceptance. These Beroean Jews could not have foreseen how many Christian groups of later days would call themselves "Beroeans" after their worthy example of Bible study. As we might expect from people who welcomed the apostolic message with such eagerness of mind, many of them believed. As at Thessalonica, the believers included many God-fearing Greeks, both men and women, and some of these—particularly the women—belonged to the leading families in the city." (F. F. Bruce, *The Book of Acts*, p. 347)

**Question 3.** "Athens was not exactly on Paul's missionary programme, and during the days that he waited there for his two friends to rejoin him, he had leisure to walk round the violet-crowned city and view its masterpieces of architecture and sculpture.

"Athens, although she had long since lost her political eminence of an earlier day, continued to represent the highest level of culture attained in classical antiquity. The sculpture, literature and oratory of Athens in the fifth and fourth centuries B.C. have, indeed, never been surpassed. In philosophy, too, she occupied the leading place, being the native city of Socrates and Plato, and the adopted home of Aristotle, Epicurus and Zeno. In all these fields Athens retained unchallenged prestige, and her political glory as the cradle of democracy was not completely dimmed. In consideration of her splendid past, the Romans left Athens free to carry on her own institutions as a free and allied city within the Roman Empire.

". . . Whatever Paul may have felt in the way of artistic appreciation, the feeling that was uppermost in his mind as he walked here and there in Athens was one of indignation: the beautiful city was 'full of idols,' dedicated to the worship of gods which were no gods—for 'the things which the Gentiles sacrifice, they sacrifice to demons and not to God' (1 Cor. 10:20)" (F. F. Bruce, *The Book of Acts*, pp. 348-49).

If it doesn't come up in discussion, you might want to point out to the group that we see continued evidence of Paul's strategy of worldwide evangelization. It is good and right to have a plan. And with a plan it is still possible to be led by the Spirit of God. (This ministry in Athens was not in Paul's original plan.) These are not opposed to each other.

It is also evident here that all truth is God's truth. In verse 28 Paul quotes a pagan poet to make one of his points.

Paul spends much of his time here in the marketplace and was even taken to a meeting of the Court of Areopagus, which "retained authority in matters of religion and morals, and in Roman times it enjoyed enhanced power and commanded great respect" (F. F. Bruce, *The Book of Acts*, pp. 352).

It was before this court that Paul was brought to give an account of his philosophy. Note that instead of beginning with Scripture, he begins with statements and items that are familiar with the people. He talks about their being religious. He mentions their objects of worship and an altar with the inscription "to an unknown god." From that point he tells them about the true living God.

**Questions 5-6.** Help the group not to gloss over these questions. As the leader, you should think through ahead of time modern objects of worship and how the message of Christ speaks to them. Some objects of worship are material goods, status, personal identity, jobs, our country, our military power and our own strength.

**Question 7.** Some "points of truth" include beginning where people might be, fear of death, non-nurturing families, "Jesus was a good man," "I am what I do" and so forth.

**Question 10.** Compromise of the gospel can be subtle and unintentional. Sometimes we are so acculturated we do not even realize the truth is being watered down. Do we communicate with conviction, though with great compassion, that repentance is essential for salvation? Is the message of the resurrected Lord proclaimed loudly and clearly? Do we skirt the issue of sin? We must not compromise the message of Jesus Christ, but we must be full of love and tenderness as we communicate this message clearly.

**Study 5. Companions in Ministry. Acts 18.**

*Purpose:* To observe the effects of relationships on Paul as he continues the task of worldwide evangelization. To be reminded of the strategic role that relationships with others play in our motivation for and efforts to evangelize.

**Question 2.** Limit the time spent on this question. This is an overview question. The passage should simply be scanned, and the people listed, giving a sense of how many people there are in Paul's life.

**Question 3.** "This married couple, whom Paul later called his 'fellow-workers in Christ Jesus', who had 'risked their lives' for him, exemplified an extraordinary degree of mobility. They left Rome for Corinth. They later undertook a further move, this time from Corinth to Ephesus in the company of Paul, and the church, or a portion of it, met in their house (18:18, 19, 26)."

"Each Jewish boy learned a trade and tried to earn his living with it. Paul and Aquila had been trained in tentmaking. As a tentmaker Paul was able to go wherever God led him carrying his livelihood with him" *(Life Application Bible,* p. 1669).

To summarize the significance of Aquila and Priscilla's relationship with Paul: they provided him a place to stay, earned a living together, possibly supported him financially (one commentator suggests that they might have financed his trip to Ephesus), traveled with him, shared their home with the church and participated in his ministry. Paul was sustained by their faithful friendship.

**Question 4.** "After a few weeks, Paul was rejoined by his colleagues Silas and Timothy. The news that they brought from Macedonia (especially Timothy's news about the steadfastness of the sorely-tried converts of Thessalonica) was a great relief to Paul; and a gift of money which they brought him from his friends in Philippi relieved him for the time being of the necessity to support himself by leather-working; he was able therefore to concentrate on the preaching of the gospel, as he sought to convince the Jewish community that Jesus was the true Messiah" F. F. Bruce, *The Book of Acts, pp. 370-71).*

Their sheer faithfulness in travel and ministry must have been a great encouragement to Paul.

**Question 8.** "Shortly after Paul left the synagogue and made the house of Titius Justus his headquarters, he had an encouraging experience—he received one of the visions which came to him at critical periods in his life, heartening him for the work that lay ahead. In this particular vision the risen Christ appeared to him by night and assured him that no harm would befall him in Corinth, for the opposition that his preaching might stir up. He should therefore abandon any fear that he might have, and go on proclaiming the gospel boldly; he would reap an abundant harvest by so doing, for the Lord had many people in Corinth whom He had marked out for His own.

"Thus filled with fresh confidence, Paul stayed in Corinth and continued his work of proclamation and teaching for eighteen months" (F. F. Bruce, *The Book of Acts,* p. 372).

**Question 9.** We have already discussed the significance of Paul's relationship with Aquila and Priscilla. Very probably his hair being cut off was also connected in some way to his relationships with people.

Concerning the vow that was made:

> The reference to his hair makes it almost certain that it was a Nazirite vow, which involved abstinence from drinking wine and from cutting one's hair for a period, at the end of which the hair was first cut and then burned, along with other sacrifices as a symbol of self-offering to God. If the vow was completed away from Jerusalem, the hair could still be brought there to be burned. Such vows were made either in thankfulness for past blessings (such as Paul's safe keeping in Corinth) or as a part of a petition for future blessings (such as safe keeping on Paul's impending journey). Once Paul had been liberated from the attempt to be justified by the law, his conscience was free to take part in practices which, being ceremonial or cultural, belonged to the matters indifferent, perhaps on this occasion in order to conciliate the Jewish Christian leaders he was going to see in Jerusalem. (John Stott, *The Spirit, the Church and the World: the Message of Acts* [Downers Grove, Ill.: InterVarsity Press, 1990], pp. 300-301)

We see his continued commitment to the Jews, though they are very difficult. In this situation they seem more responsive and even ask him to come back. He promises to do so if it is the Lord's will.

Though few words tell about it in this portion of Scripture (vv. 22-23), Paul's relationship to the church is important to them and to him. He spent time with them, shared with them and strengthened the disciples.

**Question 11.** When it was evident that Apollos' teaching was defective and that he needed more training, Aquila and Priscilla invited him to their home and explained the way of God more accurately.

"Their ministry was timely and discreet. As Professor Bruce remarks, 'how much better it is to give such private help to a preacher whose ministry is defective than to correct him or denounce him publicly!' " (John Stott, *The Spirit,* p. 296).

**Question 12.** "Next, when Apollos wanted to go to Achaia, the brothers encouraged him, for he was better equipped now for a wider ministry, and wrote to the disciples there to welcome him. On arriving, he vigorously refuted the Jews in public debate, proving from the Scriptures that Jesus was the Christ. Indeed in 1 Corinthians 1-4 Paul himself wrote appreciatively of Apollos' ministry in Corinth and generously acknowledged him as a fellow worker in God's field. 'I planted the seed,' he wrote; 'Apollos watered it, but God made it grow' " (John Stott, *The Spirit,* p. 303).

**Study 6. In the Name of Jesus. Acts 19:1—20:12.**
*Purpose:* To see the different types of reactions as the power of God is demonstrated in mighty ways. To be motivated to seek the demonstration of this power in our lives and Christian communities.
*Background:* Ephesus was the capital and leading business center of the Roman province of Asia. It is part of present-day Turkey. Because it was a hub of transportation, both sea and land, it ranked with the greatness of Antioch and Alexandria. It was a major city on the Mediterranean Sea.
**Question 1.** God's power is revealed in all sorts of ways—from his giving wisdom for dealing with a child to the miracle of the new birth to reconciliation in a broken relationship to supernatural healing. This question is simply meant to prepare the group for considering God's power and the effects of it on the world.
**Question 2.** This question is to serve as an overview of the passage. Help set the pace for just scanning the passage. However, help the group to see not just the dramatic episodes as the power of God in action, but such powerful things as a person believing in Jesus. Some of the episodes will be discussed in more detail as we move through the study.
**Question 3.** This is another overview question. Watch your time.
**Question 4.** This question should bring out the fact that Paul met a small group of people with a particular spiritual need—to receive the Holy Spirit—and effectively met that need. He began by asking sensitive questions. He started where they were, and where they had been, and then took them a step forward in their growth and spiritual experience. They were receptive and responsive.

This episode, depending on the make-up of your group, has potential for being controversial. Try to avoid the controversy and stay with what all can agree upon. The commentary material below might be helpful if controversy cannot be avoided. Even so, at some point it might be necessary for you to say, "Let's move on with our study and discuss this point after our study is over."

Some feel this text is proof that conversion occurs in steps. First there is repentance and a commitment to Jesus, and then a second step in which one receives the Holy Spirit. Others believe that this all takes place at one time with conversion. This debate cannot be settled (and minds will not be changed) in the process of this study. There are some issues where Christians have to agree to disagree and move on.

> John's baptism was a sign of repentance from sin only, not a sign of new life in Christ. Like Apollos (18:24-26), these Ephesian believers needed further instruction on the message and ministry of Jesus Christ. By faith they believed in Jesus as the Messiah, but they did not understand the significance of Jesus' death and resurrection or the work of the Holy Spirit. Therefore they had not experienced the presence and power of the Holy Spirit.
>
> In the book of Acts, believers received the Holy Spirit in a variety of ways. Usually the Holy Spirit filled a person as soon as he or she professed faith in Christ. In this case, however, God allowed it to happen later. God was confirming to these believers who did not initially know about the Holy Spirit that they too were a part of the church. The Holy Spirit's filling endorsed them as believers.
>
> Pentecost was the formal outpouring of the Holy Spirit to the church. The other outpourings

in the book of Acts were God's way of uniting new believers to the church. The mark of the true church is not merely right doctrine, but evidence of the Holy Spirit's work." *(Life Application Bible,* p. 1673)

**Question 5.** We need to ask questions more. We need to allow others to tell us where they are in their relationship with God. We need to take seriously what they share and then begin our communication from where they are and according to their openness. The disciples were ready for what Paul had to offer. He forced nothing on them. More time should be spent listening to others than talking.

**Question 6.** Paul patiently and faithfully began his ministry in the synagogue as he had in other cities. He knew the Jews at Ephesus from his previous visit when they had pressed him to stay longer. He had promised to come back if God willed. But the old patterns continued and the Jewish leaders rejected the message. Paul took up residence in a secular environment in the teaching hall of Tyrannus. Those who had accepted his message in the synagogue could follow him there.

Notice that for two full years this work went on. Paul stayed in Ephesus, but his colleagues worked out in other cities. Verse 10 says that everyone had heard the Word of God by the end of that period.

"The province was intensively evangelized, and became one of the leading centres of Christianity for centuries afterwards" (F. F. Bruce, *The Book of Acts,* p. 389).

**Question 7.** Too often we have strategies and plans for all types of things in our lives—for our jobs, homes, social lives, goals for the future and our children. But when it comes to one of the most important areas of our lives, that of evangelism, we have no such plans or strategies. What do you need to be thinking, planning and praying about concerning the spread of the gospel in your work place, in your neighborhood and in social or professional groups? How might you penetrate these with the gospel—even to the possible desired end that "all the Jews and Greeks who lived in the province of Asia heard the Word of the Lord"?

**Question 8.** It has been revealed through scrolls that "pagan" exorcisms took place using the name of Jesus. So Jesus' name was being used by those who didn't follow him—apparently just for power's sake.

**Question 13.** Just being aware that such negative responses will take place helps us not to be alarmed when it happens. For instance, it is not necessarily bad if someone gets angry when confronted with the gospel. It could mean that the message is getting through. Of course, we need to make sure the anger is not the result of an inappropriate or insensitive approach.

Knowing that truth is often copied alerts us to watch for that and warns us not to get caught up in compromise.

Being in tune with God and saturated in his Word is vital preparation. We need his wisdom and insight. We need his comfort and encouragement. We need to be reminded of his purpose and priorities.

When the response is positive, we need to give God the full credit and glory for all that is accomplished. Apart from the power of his Spirit we can do nothing.

**Study 7. Paul's Farewell. Acts 20:13-38.**

*Purpose:* To review Paul's life and to be motivated by it to strive to complete the task of testifying to God's grace.

**Question 1.** This is a dramatic, touching and emotional episode. Paul is saying goodby to people that he has loved and invested in for three intense years. He has brought them to Christ. He has nurtured and discipled them. He has turned over to them the leadership of the church at Ephesus. And now he knows and is communicating to them that they will never see his face again.

They were grieving. But because this is the last time they will see him, the power of his words increases. They will remember what Paul said. This approach question is to help the group get into the spirit and the emotion of this powerful passage.

**Question 2.** Not often do we start looking at the content of a passage with a feeling question. However, as in much of life, if not all, the feelings will enrich and emphasize the impact of the content. Scan the passage with this question, but do not rush. However, keep in mind that the content will be covered in more depth as we move through the passage.

"The meeting at Miletus between Paul and the elders of the Ephesian church is important because it contains the one record in Acts of Paul's addressing a Christian audience. The address throws light both on the course of events in the recent past and on Paul's misgivings for the future, although nothing shifted him from his determination to carry out the work divinely allotted to him and to finish his work with joy" (*The New Bible,* p. 1001).

**Question 3.** The goal of this study is to review Paul's life and to be motivated by it to strive to complete the task that God has called us to testify to the gospel of God's grace. That means the reviewing of his ministry is very important and the foundation to the rest of the study. Look at each portion carefully.

**Question 4.** Help the group to respond to this question. The best way is to be prepared to share your response to it.

The goal is not to be like Paul. It is to be us but with the same motivation and desire for obedience as Paul.

**Question 5.** Help the group to be specific.

**Questions 9-10.** "And now he was leaving them; they could no longer count upon his personal presence for such pastoral guidance and wise admonition. But, though Paul might go, God was ever with them, and so was God's word which they had received—the word that proclaimed his grace in redeeming them and His grace in sanctifying them. To God, then, and to this word of His, Paul solemnly committed them. By that word, as they accepted and obeyed it, they would be built up in faith and love together with their fellow-Christians; by that word, too, they were assured of their inheritance among all the people of God, sanctified by His grace. In due time Paul and all the apostles passed from earthly life; but the apostolic teaching which they left behind as a sacred deposit to be guarded by their successors, preserved not merely in the memory of their hearers but in the scriptures of the NT canon, remains with us this day as the Word of God's grace. And those are most truly in the apostolic succession who receive this apostolic teaching, along with the rest of Holy Writ, as their rule of faith and practice" (F. F. Bruce, *The Book of Acts,* pp. 417-18).

**Question 11.** You might begin this question with a statement about the importance of the job you are called to do.

> Upon these elders, then lay a solemn responsibility. The Holy Spirit had entrusted them with the charge of the people of God in Ephesus: they had to care for them as shepherds for their flock.

. . . Their responsibility was all the greater in that the congregation of God which He had purchased for Himself (an echo this of O.T. language)—and the ransom price was nothing less than the life-blood of his beloved son. (F. F. Bruce, *The Book of Acts,* pp. 415-16)

**Study 8. Facing Opposition. Acts 21:1—22:21.**

*Purpose:* To seek for our life the singlemindedness of Paul in obedience to God's will.

**Question 3.** Paul did not disobey the Holy Spirit by going to Jerusalem (v. 4). The Spirit warned the believers about what Paul would suffer there, and they decided he should not go because of that. In the same way the people in verse 12 begged him not to go after hearing the prophecy from Agabus.

Paul knew that he would be imprisoned in Jerusalem. Though no one wants to endure pain, as a faithful disciple Paul wanted above all else to obey God.

You might also ask, "What was the source of his resolve (v. 13)?" It is important to note that his resolve centered upon the name of the Lord Jesus Christ.

**Question 6.** "When the delegates called on James and the elders of the Jerusalem church they were welcomed; but these good men were clearly troubled because of the exaggerated rumours that had reached Jerusalem about Paul's attitude to the law. They admitted that the position with regard to Gentile believers had been defined at the apostolic Council, but they wished Paul to give the lie in a practical manner to the report that he was dissuading Jewish Christians from keeping the law and from circumcising their children. Paul himself, so far as we can tell, continued to observe the law throughout his life, especially in Jewish company, and his consent to take the advice of James on this occasion and share the purificatory ceremony of four men who had taken a temporary Nazirite vow and pay their expenses was entirely in keeping with his settled principle: 'To the Jews I became as a Jew, in order to win Jews' " *(The New Bible,* p. 1002).

**Question 7.** "The Jerusalem Council (Acts 15) settled the issue of circumcision of Gentile believers. Evidently there was a rumor that Paul had gone far beyond their decision, even forbidding Jews to circumcise their children. This, of course, was not true. So Paul willingly submitted to Jewish custom to show that he was not working against the council's decision and that he was still Jewish in his lifestyle. Sometimes we must go the second mile to avoid offending others, especially when offending them would hinder the gospel.

"Paul submitted himself to this Jewish custom to keep peace in the Jerusalem church. Although Paul was a man of strong conviction, he was willing to compromise on nonessential points, becoming all things to all men that he might win some (1 Corinthians 9:19-23). Often a church will split on disagreements about minor issues or traditions. Like Paul, we should remain firm on Christian essentials but flexible on nonessentials. This is exercising the gift of mutual submission for the sake of the gospel" *(Life Application Bible,* p. 1680).

**Question 8.** "It was a remarkable feat of intellectual balance and self-control after the violence of the mob's man handling, and a rescue which can have taken little thought of gentleness, to lay hold of the opportunity for testimony, and in the act assess the needs of the situation and the appropriate approach. Paul casts aside all theology and bases his defense on the facts of personal experience. In spite of the stinging injustice he had suffered, and the ungodly violence of the crowd's attack from which he was still reeling, he does all he possibly can do to conciliate his hostile audience" (R. V. G. Tasker, *The Acts,* p. 173).

**Question 10.** Consider such things as respect, honesty and straightforwardness, identification with the listeners, lifting Jesus up.

Bible translators disagree as to whether Paul was speaking Aramaic or Hebrew. However, as Aramaic is derived from Hebrew and was the primary language of Palestinian Jews *(The NIV Study Bible,* p. 1689) the following comments are helpful in any case:

> Paul was speaking in Hebrew, the language of the Old Testament. He spoke this language not only to communicate in the language of his listeners, but also to show that he was a devout Jew, had respect for the Jewish laws and customs and was learned in Hebrew. Paul spoke Greek to the Roman officials and Hebrew to the Jews. If you want to minister to people with maximum effectiveness, you must be able to use their language.
>
> Gamaliel was the most honored rabbi of the first century. He was well known and respected as an expert on religious law and as a voice for moderation. Paul was showing his credentials as a well-educated man trained under the most respected Jewish rabbi.
>
> When Paul said "just as you have tried to do today (i.e., as any of you are today [NIV])" he acknowledged their sincere motives in trying to kill him and recognized that he would have done the same to Christian leaders a few years earlier. Paul always tried to establish a common point of contact with his audience before launching into a full-scale defense of Christianity. *(Life Application Bible,* p. 1681)

He postpones the name Gentile as long as possible demonstrating a sensitivity to his audience. He even modifies the Lord's words in verse 15 (Acts 9:15).

"He was bound to speak, however, to speak the whole truth, and there came a place in his address, as there did at Athens, when no art of oratory or grace of language could cover up the point of thrust of the speaker's challenge" (R. V. G. Tasker, pp. 173-74).

**Study 9. God at Work. Acts 22:22—23:35.**

*Purpose:* To see God's hand in the life of Paul directing and protecting him in order for God's will to be done. To become more astute at seeing God's hand in our lives and circumstances.

**Question 2.** It is God's will for Paul to go to Rome. He is faithfully working this out by both protecting and directing Paul.

"Twice more in this brief section Roman law and justice come to Paul's aid. First Claudius Lysias again rescues him from lynching, and secondly, having discovered his Roman citizenship, from flogging.

"Paul was actually being prepared for the flogging when he divulged his Roman citizenship. Similarly, in Philippi he had not revealed that he was a Roman citizen until after he had been beaten, imprisoned and put in the stocks (16:31). He seems for some reason not to have wanted to take advantage of being a citizen except in some dire extremity" (John Stott, *The Spirit,* p. 348).

**Question 3.** The disagreement between the Sadducees and the Pharisees and the uproar that it caused led to Paul's being swooped away to protection by the commander.

**Question 4.** "It is true that the event on the Damascus road shattered and rebuilt Paul's life. Never was conversion so complete and so transforming. But it is also correct to say, as Ramsay maintains that, when Paul came to look over the whole course of his life, and to reflect calmly on the plan which was so clearly woven into it, he saw the continuity and unfolding purpose to which he often makes reference. He had been separated, he claims, from his mother's womb for the task before him. 'Brethren,' he said, 'I have lived in all good conscience before God until this day' " (R. V. G. Tasker, *The Acts,* pp. 175-76). Paul was claiming to be serving God sincerely and without offense. His life had been consistently directed to one end—glorifying the God of Israel.

**Question 6.** Paul was spared from the plot by the Jews to kill him because of the information brought to him by his nephew.

> On the one hand, the Jewish persecutors were prejudiced and violent. On the other, the Romans were open-minded and went out of their way to maintain the standards of law, justice and order of which their best leaders were understandably proud. Four times they rescued Paul from death either by lynching or murder, taking him into custody until the charges against him could be clarified and, if cogent, presented in court. Then three times in Luke's narrative, as we have seen, Paul either has been or will be declared innocent. *(The Spirit,* p. 356)

**Question 7.** "Paul had passed through two days of fearful mental, spiritual, and physical stress. Twice the intervention of a Roman military patrol had rescued him from the violence of his own compatriots. He was no doubt assailed with misgivings, and the recollection of the warnings which had punctuated his journey to Jerusalem would arise to torment him" (R. V. G. Tasker, *The Acts,* p. 177). He needed God's voice of comfort and encouragement.

**Question 9.** "Lysias somewhat manipulated the facts in order to portray himself in the most favourable light, putting his discovery that Paul was a Roman citizen before his rescue instead of after it, and drawing a discreet veil of silence over his serious offence in binding, and preparing to torture, a Roman citizen. Nine of the principal verbs in his letter are in the first person singular. The letter was fairly honourable, but decidedly self-centered" (John Stott, *The Spirit,* p. 356).

**Study 10. Falsely Accused. Acts 24:1—25:12.**

*Purpose:* To learn from Paul how to respond when falsely accused due to our faith.

**Question 1.** If you don't get much response—or if the responses don't seem realistic—as a follow-up, you might try, "What if the accusations are made over and over again?"

**Question 2.** "The charges made followed those levelled against Christ Himself, and fall similarly under three heads. First, Paul was *a pestilent* fellow, and a mover of sedition among all the Jews throughout the world (5). This amounted to a charge of treason, or *laesa maiestas.* This crime lacked precise definition in Roman law, and became a device under tyrannical emperors for political terrorism. Authoritarian regimes have at all times been noted for the employment of elastic legal safeguards of the sort. In days of good government the law of treason found no exercise, but it was always prone to revival. . . . Secondly, Paul was set down as a ring-leader of the Nazarenes, a group without official recognition, and by implication dissident and rebellious. Finally, he had profaned the temple, the one charge on which the Jews appear to have been able even to put a Roman to death. Tertullus backed his accusations with the testimony of eyewitnesses (9)" (R. V. G. Tasker, *The Acts,* p. 180).

**Question 3.** "A few words only of Tertullus' elaborate oration are given, but enough to reveal the nature of this rhetoric and the character of his accusation. Luke has a remarkable aptitude for using thus a brief quotation. It is not unlikely that the orator was a Roman, for there is a Latin ring about some of his phrases as they appear in Luke's Greek, and his name, although this does not necessarily indicate nationality, is Latin. He was certainly trained in the arts of contemporary rhetoric, and what impressed Luke was his elaborate exorduim, a *captatio benevolentiae,* or 'seeking of good will,' as the theorists termed it. Such a subterfuge, says Calvin, is 'a sign of bad conscience' " (R. V. G. Tasker, *The Acts,* p. 179).

**Question 5.** This is a speculative question, though certainly worth thinking about. That is why the words "What do you think *might* have been?" are used.

"Felix had been governor for six years and would have known about the Christians, a topic of conversation among the Roman leaders. The Christians' peaceful lifestyles had shown the Romans that Christians didn't go around starting riots" *(Life Application Bible,* p. 1686).

**Question 6.** It would seem that Paul's message got too personal and Felix fell under conviction. Felix had taken another man's wife. When Paul spoke on righteousness, self-control and judgment he became uncomfortable and ended the discussion. There is no evidence that it ever became convenient for Felix to further discuss Christianity.

**Question 7.** When exposed to truth that reveals sin, some people move further away, even as some are moved by the Holy Spirit to respond in repentance. They might say, as Felix did, "When it is more convenient, I will consider the gospel." That time usually does not come.

"Many people will be glad to discuss the gospel with you as long as it doesn't touch their lives too personally. When it does some will resist or run away. But this is what the gospel is all about—God's power to change lives" *(Life Application Bible,* p. 1686).

The gospel's real effectiveness is when it moves from principles and doctrine into a life-changing dynamic. When someone resists or runs from your witness, it is possibly because the gospel has become personal.

**Question 12.** "Striving to keep our conscience clear before God and man" is a vital element in responding to false accusation.

**Study 11. Paul Before Agrippa. Acts 25:13—26:32.**

*Purpose:* To make Paul's burning desire that each person will hear the gospel and will become a Christian our own.

**Question 2.** "A fresh difficulty now presented itself to Festus. When he sent Paul to Rome to have his case heard before the emperor, it would be necessary for him to send a report of the case as it had developed up to that time. This was by no means an easy thing to do, especially as Festus could not grasp how the trouble had really started. Listening to the speeches for the prosecution and the defence only added to his perplexity.

"Fortunately for Festus, a way out of this minor difficulty soon appeared. To the north-east of his province lay the petty kingdom which was ruled by Herod Agrippa II. . . .

"Agrippa the younger had the reputation of being an authority on the Jewish religion, and Festus decided that he was the man who could best help him to frame the report which he had to remit to Rome in connection with Paul's appeal to the emperor. So at the suitable opportunity during Agrippa's stay in the provincial capital, Festus broached the subject of Paul's case to him" (F. F. Bruce, *The Book of Acts,* pp. 481-82).

Knowing Paul was innocent and observing the power of Paul's message ate away at Festus. He could not help but talk about it.

**Question 3.** I believe Festus's report to Agrippa shows us some of Festus's response to Paul.

It is significant that Paul made an impression on Festus. Though it is important to him to stay on the "good side" of the Jews, he was not ready to ignore Paul's innocence. He was willing to admit to another leader that he did not know what to do. His report made Agrippa want to hear from Paul.

There are many times we may think our witness has no effect. Sometimes, even though we cannot see what is going on with people's inner lives, God is working in them through us.

**Question 4.** Festus says that the issue of controversy seemed to be one Jesus who was dead but whom Paul affirmed to be alive.

**Question 6.** "Agrippa no doubt knew enough about the Christian movement to have his interest whetted by Festus" (F. F. Bruce, *The Book of Acts,* p. 482).

**Question 11.** "Paul to Agrippa (boldly confronting the king, of whom he has just been speaking to Festus in the third person): 'King Agrippa, do you believe the prophets? I know you do' (27).

"The court gasps. Has any prisoner ever before presumed to address his Royal Highness with such impertinence? Agrippa is unhorsed. Too embarrassed to give Paul a direct answer to a direct question, and too proud to allow him to dictate the topic of their dialogue, he takes evasive action with an ambiguous counter-question.

"Agrippa to Paul: 'Do you think that in such a short time you can persuade me to be a Christian?' (28).

"The court gasps again. That was a clever riposte, by which the king regained the initiative. A murmur went round the audience as people discussed exactly what he meant. It was 'variously represented as a trivial jest, a bitter sarcasm, a grave irony, a burst of anger, and an expression of *sincere conviction.*' How would Paul respond?

"Paul to Agrippa (in no doubt how he will interpret the king's words, and determined to exploit them for the gospel): 'Short time or long—I pray God that not only you but all who are listening to me today may become what I am, except for these chains' (29).

"With those words Paul lifted his hands and rattled the chains which bound him. He was sincere, the prisoner Paul. He really believed what he was talking about. He wanted everybody to be like him, including the king—everybody a Christian, but nobody a prisoner. You could not help admiring his integrity. There was also a finality about his statement, for his judges had nothing more to say" (John Stott, *The Spirit,* pp. 376-77).

**Study 12. Paul in Rome! Acts 27—28.**

*Purpose:* To rejoice in Paul's reaching Rome and to have our confidence in God so affected by what he did in Paul's life that we go forth "boldly and without hindrance proclaiming the kingdom of God and teaching others about the Lord Jesus Christ." (Acts 28:31)

**General Note:** I would urge you to lead the group in taking seriously the truth not only of these last two chapters but of the whole book of Acts. A quick summary might be appropriate. Be prepared to do such if you feel it will be helpful.

Try to help members to see the excitement of God's fulfilling his purpose. Against all odds, he has gotten Paul to Rome. Also, look at Paul's great faithfulness to God and his singleness of mind in proclaiming the gospel of Jesus Christ.

Whether or not you have prayed together before, I would highly recommend a time of prayer at the end of this study.

**Question 1.** Remember this is just an approach question. Not a lot of time should be spent on it. Be on guard so that the discussion does not get too philosophical and thus too lengthy. There are many important things to cover in this last study.

**Question 2.** "So far in the Acts Luke has depicted Paul as the apostle to the Gentiles, the pioneer of the three missionary expeditions, the prisoner, and the defendant. Now, however, he portrays him in a different light. He is no longer an honoured apostle, but an ordinary man among men, a lonely Christian (apart from Luke himself and Aristarchus) among nearly three hundred non-Christians, who were either soldiers or prisoners or perhaps merchants or crew. Yet Paul's God-given leadership gifts clearly emerge. 'It is quite certain', writes William Barclay, 'that Paul was the most experienced traveller on board that ship.' Even Haenchen, who scornfully dismisses Luke's portrait of him as 'only . . . a mighty superman', concedes that Luke fails to draw our attention adequately to Paul's expertise as a seasoned seafarer. He catalogues the apostle's eleven voyages on the Mediterranean before he set sail for Rome and calculates that Paul had travelled at least 3,500 miles by sea. Yet it was more than mature experience at sea which made Paul stand out as a leader on board ship; it was *his steadfast Christian faith and character*" (John Stott, *The Spirit,* p. 390).

This is an important question. It is an overview of the passage, which is long, and focuses on its important content. Look carefully at all the ways Paul ministers to others.

**Question 3.** It seems to me that each time Paul ministered it was out of compassion—whether it was warning the ship leaders of loss of life and cargo (he could have just taken care of himself) (27:9-10), letting them be comforted by God's promise of safety (27:21-25) instead of keeping that to himself, encouraging them to take nourishment, stay on the ship or building them a fire in order to care for their bodies (27:31-38; 28:31), healing the islanders (28:8-9), or sharing the gospel with the Jews (28:17-20, 23-31).

**Question 4.** Julius trusted Paul and desired to be kind to him. Julius must have seen in Paul the character of Christ, his integrity and that he was a man worth being kind to. Paul built relationships wherever he was that honored the Lord and that communicated to people their value—even those taking him to prison and guarding him.

**Question 5.** "At all events, he now had complete confidence in what he was about to say. Twice he urged them to keep up their courage (22, 25). On what ground? Because none of them, he said, but only the ship, would be lost (22). How could he be so certain? Because the previous night an angel of the God to whom he belonged, and whom he served, had stood beside him (23), had told him not to be afraid, had promised that he must without fail stand trial before Caesar, and had added that God would give him (in answer to his prayers?) the lives of all his fellow passengers (24). These divine promises were the foundation of Paul's summons to everybody to maintain their courage. For he believed in God, in his character and covenant, and was convinced that he would keep his promises (25), even though the first ship would have to run aground on some island (26)" (John Stott, *The Spirit,* p. 392).

**Question 6.** There were many ways people were affected by Paul's confidence in God. All of Paul's being was permeated with Christ. Thus, people were affected by his lifestyle, not just his preaching. Consider the broad scope of the effect of his ministry. This question is meant to prepare your group for question 9 as well as questions 7 and 8.

**Question 9.** Questions 7 and 8 bring out the effect that our confidence in God has on our witness of the claims of Christ to non-Christian friends. Help your group to think through how people are affected by our confidence in God to meet the physical, spiritual and emotional needs of ourselves and others.

---

*Phyllis Le Peau is the mother of four, a registered nurse and a former Nurses Christian Fellowship staffworker. Currently, she is assistant program director for Wellness, Inc. Phyllis is also the author of the Caring People Bible Studies (IVP) and has coauthored several LifeGuide® Bible Studies with her husband, Andy.*